Sacramental Theology

A GENERAL INTRODUCTION

KENAN B. OSBORNE, O.F.M.

PAULIST PRESS
New York ● *Mahwah*

Library of Congress Cataloging-in-Publication Data

Osborne, Kenan B.
    Sacramental theology.

    Bibliography: p.
    Includes index.
    1. Sacraments—Catholic Church. 2. Catholic
Church—Doctrines. 3. Catholic Church—Liturgy.
I. Title.
BX2200.077 1988   234'.16   87–25906
ISBN 0-8091-2945-0 (pbk.)

Published by Paulist Press
997 Macarthur Boulevard
Mahwah, N.J. 07430

Printed and bound in the United States of America

CONTENTS

CHAPTER ONE
Current Roman Catholic Theology of the Sacraments   1

CHAPTER TWO
The Naming and Function of Sacrament   20

CHAPTER THREE
Methodology and the Christian Sacraments   33

CHAPTER FOUR
God's Action in the Sacramental Event   49

CHAPTER FIVE
Jesus as Primordial Sacrament   69

CHAPTER SIX
The Church as a Basic Sacrament   86

CHAPTER SEVEN
Official Church Teaching on the Sacraments   100

CHAPTER EIGHT
Sacraments and Christian Spirituality   119

Epilogue   139
Notes   142
Bibliography   151
Index   153

DEDICATED TO
Franciscan Friars
Province of St. Barbara

Chapter One

Current Roman Catholic Theology of the Sacraments

ONE OF THE MAJOR AREAS OF THEOLOGICAL DISCUSSION IN the Roman Catholic Church during the past century has been that of sacramental theology. This renewed discussion of the sacraments has had effects not only on the academic and theological life of the Church, but also on the practical and liturgical life of the Church. Since the Second Vatican Council all the rites of the sacraments have been renewed, with the result that the celebration of these sacraments in Catholic churches throughout the world has taken on profound changes. One might even say that in this past century a fairly revolutionary approach in sacramental theology and sacramental life has occurred in the Catholic Church. This in no way means that tradition has been abolished, since in many cases it is precisely the tradition which has been reconsidered and revivified.

In this opening chapter on current Roman Catholic theology of the sacraments, we will consider the main factors which occasioned the renewal. Such factors are the following:

1. Scholarly research into the history of the sacraments.
2. The development of the Church and the humanity of Jesus as sacraments.

1

3. The ecumenical movement.
4. Liberation theology.

Before we consider each of these factors, it should be recalled that a study of the sacraments has many presuppositions. First of all, there is an ecclesiology which undergirds any theology and practice of sacraments. Undergirding the theology, on the other hand, is a Christology which shapes one's understanding of Church. This Christology, therefore, is a second presupposition. A third presupposition involves the way in which one interprets the Scriptures, particularly the New Testament. A fundamentalist interpretation will act in one way as a presupposition, whereas an historical-critical interpretation will act in a different way as a presupposition. Such presuppositions are not the focus of this book, and therefore will not be expressly treated. From a practical standpoint, difficulties or differences in sacramental theology and/or practice often are insoluble if one remains only at the sacramental level. To solve such differences, one must face the ecclesiological differences and the Christological differences. This is particularly evident at a diocesan or parish level, in which differences regarding baptism, confirmation, etc., begin to emerge. These differences might be better resolved if the ecclesiological or Christological problems were openly surfaced and discussed. The same problem of differences and resolution of such differences occurs in ecumenical dialogues. Here, too, ecclesiological issues, rather than sacramental issues might easily be the source of friction, and therefore must be openly confronted.

1. Scholarly Research into the History of the Sacraments

In 1896 at Philadelphia, Henry Charles Lea published his three-volume work on *A History of Auricular Confession and*

Indulgences in the Latin Church.[1] It was a massive work of scholarship, but heavily anti-Catholic. In many ways, this work occasioned the beginning of contemporary study into the history of the sacraments, not that there had not been historical studies prior to 1896, but that after this work such studies took on a less sporadic form and a much more concerted and deliberate form. In 1896, however, the Catholic Church was not well-equipped to address all the issues which Lea presented. In fact, a French canonist, A. Boudinhon, was the first to reply to Lea; he did this in a lengthy article on the history of the sacrament of penance down to the eighth century: "Sur l'histoire de la pénitence. À propos d'un livre récent."[2] More scholarly and more detailed studies were, however, needed. F. X. Funk,[3] P. Battifol,[4] E. F. Vacandard,[5] and P. A. Kirsch[6] published solid historical works on the subject of the history of the sacrament of penance, and the Protestant, F. Loofs,[7] in 1906 also wrote on the subject and aligned himself more with the Catholic authors than with Lea. Nonetheless, all of these authors in many ways tended to agree with Lea on some basic historical interpretations; their works were, in part, by no means a refutation but a substantiation.

Catholic dogma professors reacted both to Lea and to the writings of their own Catholic historians in a highly negative way, defending the more or less Scholastic teaching with which they were familiar. Professors such as Gartmeier in Germany[8] and Pignataro[9] and Di Dario[10] in Italy wrote monographs in which egregious historical errors were put forward as truth, and all of this in defense of the status quo. The First World War brought a pause, of course, to any scholarship, and it was only after the peace that a new group of scholars approached the subject of the history of the sacrament of penance, namely, such authors as P. Galtier,[11] B. Poschmann,[12] A. D'Ales,[13] K. Adam,[14] J. A. Jungmann,[15] and K. Rahner.[16] In the writings of these authors, and many others, a more balanced and clarified approach to the history of the sacrament of penance has developed.

Since the sacrament of penance is seen as the sacrament of reconciliation after baptism, the "second plank of salvation," as it has been called, Catholic scholars (and non-Catholic scholars, too) began to study baptism and its history. Since baptism is the door to the Eucharist, studies on the history of the Eucharist began to appear. Such historical studies demanded a history of the ordained priesthood, since it is the ordained priest who administers baptism, generally, and penance and Eucharist, *de rigueur*. The history of baptism raised the issue of the history of confirmation, and that too became a focus of scholarly study. These five sacraments have received the lion's share of historical research. The sacrament of marriage and its history is still being developed; the history of the anointing of the sick is clearly the junior partner in all of this work.

The renewal of the sacraments, mandated by Vatican II, was done by professionals who were well aware of these historical studies, and the new ritual clearly evidences a sensitivity to the historical background of each sacrament. This is the reason why one can say that in the renewal something revolutionary has taken place, but in this revolution tradition has indeed been respected. It is the recovery of the history that is at one and the same time revolutionary and traditional.

Besides the new rites of the sacraments, approved by the Church's highest authorities, there are many books on the sacraments in our contemporary period which enjoy both great popularity and great respect: W. Bausch's volume, *A New Look at the Sacraments*[17] and J. Martos' *Doors to the Sacred*[18] come readily to mind. Many other volumes could also be cited. Such history of the individual sacraments, it must be remembered, was unavailable to the great Scholastic theologians such as St. Thomas and St. Bonaventure. This history was likewise unknown at the time of the Reformation. The Catholic Counter-Reformation was a period of defense and apologetics, and although D. Petau[19] and J. Morin[20] in the seventeenth century did publish some historical volumes on the sacraments, the historical effort they attempted to inspire in the Catholic Church had no sequel until the revival after Lea, described above. We are dealing clearly with a twentieth century phenomenon, and this phenomenon has been one of the principal factors in the renewal of sacramental theology in the Catholic Church today. Nor can one say that the historical research in any or all of the sacraments has come to an end. Scholars are continuing to put together the details in the history of the Christian sacraments.

On the basis of reliable, historical scholarship which we are privileged to enjoy today, we can say that clear, historical, extant data on each of the sacraments allows the following picture:

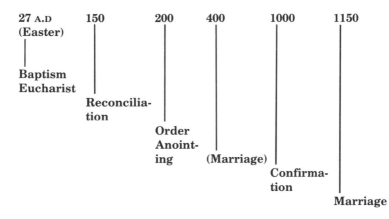

The actual dates are generalized. Baptism and Eucharist clearly go back to the time of Jesus and there is data for this in the New Testament itself. It is with the writings of Hermes (140–150) that we have the first clear reference to a rite of reconciliation after baptism. It is with the *Apostolic Tradition* of Hippolytus (c. 215) that we have the first extant ordination ritual and a clear indication of ordination. In the same work we have the first clear indication of a blessing of oil for the sick. Around 400 we begin to see, on reliable historical data, that the Church officials begin to enter into the marriage rite. Since it was not until the time of Peter Lombard in the twelfth century that theologians acknowledged marriage as a sacrament, the first indication of marriage is placed in parentheses, indicating only a first step around 400 and a clear sacramental acceptance only in the twelfth century. The year 1000 for confirmation indicates that at that time, generally in the West, a separate rite, called confirmation, can be found. Prior to 1000, in the West, less generalized situations on a separate rite of confirmation can be historically found.

This time-frame represents only the historical data on the sacraments. Theology must take into account such historical data, and it is precisely this interfacing of history and dogma which undergirds today's renewal of the sacraments. One sees, however, that the phrase in the definition of a sacrament, which has been so popular since the Council of Trent onward, namely, that a sacrament is an external sign instituted by Christ to give grace, is challenged in no small degree by the historical findings on each of the sacraments. If there is no historical evidence for a sacrament beyond a certain date, how can such a sacrament be considered as "instituted by Christ"? At this juncture, it is necessary only to perceive the problem of institution, not to solve it. Further data is needed for any effort at resolution, and this will be considered later on.

In any consideration of the history of the Christian sacraments, it must be remembered that the reality of sacramental life and action in the Church preceded any theoretical or theological discussion of sacraments. In other words, long before the Church had developed a "definition" of sacrament, the Church had been living the sacraments. Sacramental theology, then, is a reflection on an already lived Church experience. It was actually not until the eleventh and twelfth centuries that a definition of sacrament was finally arrived at, but the Church's experience of sacramental life begins with the very origin of the Church.

In the patristic period of Church history, i.e., from 100 to 700 A.D., the terms "mysterion" and "sacramentum" were used in a rather sweeping way. No technical term for sacrament had, as yet, been established, but as one moves into the period, 1000 to 1150 A.D., a technical and theological use of the term "sacrament" began to evolve in the West more so than in the East. This technical term revolved around three items:

1. Sacrament means sign or symbol. This aspect of sacramentality owes much to St. Augustine and the Augustinian tradition in Western theology. A sacrament is a visible sign, a perceptible symbol of something invisible and sacred.

2. The invisible or sacred reality, to which the sign bears witness, is grace: God's free gift of his love to men and women.

3. In the Christian Church, these sacraments or signs were not arbitrary, but stem from God's own revelation in Jesus. In other words, Jesus, in some way or another, instituted these Christian sacraments.

These three elements formed the main structure of the technical or theological "definition" of sacrament in the eleventh and twelfth centuries. For instance, Hugh of St. Victor attempted an early definition of sacrament, when he wrote: "Sacramentum est corporale vel materiale elementum foris sensibiliter propositum ex similitudine repraesentans, et ex institutione significans, et ex sanctificatione continens aliquam invisibilem et spiritualem gratiam." (A sacrament is a corporal or material element, proposed in a sensibly perceptible way, representative on the basis of its likeness, significative on the basis of its institution, and incorporative on the basis of its holiness of some invisible and spiritual grace" (*De sacramentis christianae fidei,* 1, 9, 2). This approach, as one notes, continues to be sharpened, until one arrives at that well-known definition: Sacraments are external signs instituted by Christ to give grace.

This definition was developed *before* the number of seven sacraments had been established. In the eleventh century, the Church had developed:

1. Baptism: this was a ritual, which by then was administered ordinarily to infants and was connected strongly to the theory of original sin. Consequently, the grace that was given in baptism removed one from the state of original sin and brought one into the family of God.

2. Confirmation: by the eleventh century, confirmation, in the West, but not in the East, had been separated from baptism, and was administered around the age of ten. Influential men, such as Hincmar, the bishop of Rheims, had already begun to describe this ritual as a rite in which one begins to be a soldier of Christ.

3. Eucharist: there was no doubt that the Eucharist was a sacred ritual in the Church and was traced back to the Last Supper. The real presence of Jesus in the bread and wine was central to eucharistic belief and eucharistic theology. A theory of transubstantiation, at the beginning of the eleventh century, was only in its initial or embryonic stage of development.

4. Penance: the Celtic form of penance, which was a penitential ritual which could be received frequently in life and was done in a fairly private not a public way, had, by the eleventh century, generally though not completely supplanted the Roman form of penance, which was public and administered only once in a Christian lifetime.

5. Anointing: by the eleventh century, anointing had become a priestly function. Earlier, lay men and women had administered this sacrament. However, during the Carolingian reformation, anointing of the sick and dying had been associated with the forgiveness of sins, which was reserved to priests alone. As one moves into the eleventh and twelfth centuries, anointing more and more becomes a "sacrament" of the dying.

6. Ordination: by the eleventh century ordination, not

only for priests and deacons, but also for subdiaconate and for the many minor orders, was generally considered a "sacrament." The consecration of a bishop was not considered a "sacrament" by many theologians and canonists.

These six rituals, then, were seen as "sacraments," fitting into the general definition of sacrament mentioned above. Marriage, though a ritual, was not considered a sacrament, since the issue of sexuality posed a problem for theologians. How could sexuality be a means of grace? This was the problem which at first presented itself in the issue of marriage and had to be theologically explained. In other words, we see that the definition of sacrament antedates the theological understanding of "seven sacraments." There is no intrinsic connection between the Christian definition of sacrament, on the one hand, and the number seven, on the other. This separation of the definition of "sacrament" from the number "seven" helps us understand why Luther and Calvin used the same definition of sacrament in the sixteenth century, but restricted it to only two Church rituals: baptism and Eucharist. It also helps us understand why, in the twentieth century, theologians as well as Vatican Council II could go beyond the number seven, with the Church and the humanity of Jesus brought into the theological consideration of "sacrament."

The Protestants used the same definition, but when it came to the issue of the "institution by Jesus," the Protestants maintained that the New Testament in a clear way only attested to baptism and Eucharist. Still, they argued from the very same definition which the Catholics used; the argument between Catholic and Protestant was not over a definition of sacrament but over the extent of this definition, based on New Testament data.

In the twentieth century, the inclusion of the Church and the humanity of Jesus into sacramental theology could only be done on the basis that the number seven was not intrinsically connected with the definition of sacrament. We will consider this new, twentieth century view of sacramentality in subsequent chapters.

2. The Development of the Church and the Humanity of Jesus as Sacraments

We move now to a second factor in contemporary Catholic theology which has influenced strongly the renewal of sacramental theology, namely, the inclusion of the Church and the humanity of Jesus as sacraments. There is an interesting history to this development. It would seem that the theologian who first moved in this direction in any substantial way was Otto Semmelroth, a Jesuit born in 1912 and teaching, after ordination, at the Hochschule Sankt Georgen in Frankfurt, Germany. In 1953 he published a work entitled *Die Kirche als Ursakrament* (*The Church as Original Sacrament*).[21] Karl Rahner had previously spoken of the Church as a "radical sacrament" in a multi-copied manuscript on penance. Semmelroth refers to this mimeographed document. Nonetheless, Semmelroth deserves the credit for making this term theologically acceptable. His writings, however, might have remained only for a few theological experts in Germany to discuss, with the result that the notion of the Church as a basic sacrament might have gone nowhere. It was Karl Rahner and Edward Schillebeeckx who prevented this. Rahner in 1961 published his small work, *Kirche und Sakrament;*[22] Schillebeeckx in 1960 published his work, *Christus, Sacrament van de Godsontmoeting* (*Christ the Sacrament of the Encounter with God*).[23] It was this latter work which was translated into many languages and was read so widely by the Catholic world just prior to Vatican II.

The idea of the Church as a basic sacrament makes no sense, in the writings of all these theologians, unless Jesus, in his humanity, is also seen as a fundamental or primordial sacrament. The two are understandable only in their mutuality, so that one really cannot accept Jesus as the primordial sacrament unless one also accepts the Church as a basic sacrament, and the Church as a sacrament presupposes Jesus as the primordial sacrament.

In the documents of Vatican II we find that the bishops have accepted the understanding of the Church as a basic sacrament. Seven times explicitly, and once equivalently, the documents state that the Church is to be considered as a basic sacrament:

Lumen Gentium: The Dogmatic Constitution on the Church

Art. 1: "By her relationship with Christ, the Church is a kind of sacrament or sign of intimate union with God and of the unity of all mankind. She is also an instrument for the achieving of such union and unity."

Art. 9: "God has gathered together as one all those who in faith look upon Jesus as the author of salvation and the source of unity and peace and has established them as the Church, that for each and all she may be the visible sacrament of this saving unity." St. Cyprian is cited here, who wrote in Ep. 69,9 that the Church was an "inseparabile unitatis sacramentum" (an indivisible sacrament of unity).

Art. 48: "Rising from the dead (Rom 6:9), he sent his life-giving Spirit upon his disciples and through this Spirit has established his body, the Church, as the universal sacrament of salvation."

Gaudium et Spes

Art. 45: "For every benefit which the people of God during its earthly pilgrimage can offer to the human family stems from the fact that the Church is the 'universal sacrament of salvation,' simultaneously manifesting and exercising the mystery of God's love for man."

Sacrosanctum Concilium

Art. 2: Equivalently stated, but the word sacrament is missing: "The Church is essentially both human and divine, visible but endowed with invisible realities, zealous in action and dedicated to contemplation, present in the world, but as a pilgrim, so constituted that in her the human is directed toward and subordinated to the divine, the visible to the invisible, action to contemplation, and this present world to that city yet to come, the object of our quest."

Art. 5: "For it was from the side of Christ as he slept the sleep of death upon the cross that there came forth 'the wondrous sacrament of the whole Church.' " The citation has reference to St. Augustine and a prayer from the former Roman missal.

Art. 26: "Liturgical services are not private functions but are celebrations of the Church which is 'the sacrament of unity,' namely, 'the holy people united and arranged under their bishops.' " Reference is made to St. Cyprian, *ibid.*

Ad Gentes

Art. 5: "The Lord, who had received all power in heaven and on earth (Mt 28:18), founded his Church as the sacrament of salvation."

Nowhere does the Council define this use of "sacrament," and thus we might say that the bishops in a cautious but nonetheless determined way applied the term sacrament to Church, leaving it up to theologians and others to further determine its precise meaning and its relationship to the seven sacraments. Nowhere at all do the Vatican II documents refer to Jesus as the primordial sacrament. We are, then, able to say that the Church as a sacrament is the ordinary teaching of the magisterium from Vatican II onward, and that the understanding of Jesus as a sacrament remains a theological position and no more. Still, since the two are so interrelated, a theological discussion of the Church as sacrament implies that Jesus in his humanity is also a sacrament, and vice versa. Technically, however, the distinction between a magisterial statement and a theological position remains valid.[24]

One sees in this kind of extension of "sacrament" that the popular understanding of sacrament, referred to above, namely, "an external sign, instituted by Christ to give grace," is even further strained as a working definition of sacrament. The Church might be seen as an "external sign instituted by Christ to give grace," but the humanity of Jesus in no way can be considered "an external sign instituted by himself to give grace." Moreover, if Jesus is the primordial sacrament, then the definition of sacrament will be found primordially in him, not in the Church nor in the seven rituals. In this view, Jesus determines the nature of sacrament, not the rituals.

That the Church is officially searching for a wider understanding of sacrament is also evident in the new Code of Canon Law. In the former Code (1915) canon 731 clearly employs the definition mentioned above: "All the sacraments of the new law, instituted by our Lord Christ, are special means of sanctification and salvation." In the new Code, however, we find some nuancing. In canon 840 (the counterpart of 731 above) we read:

> The sacraments of the New Testament, instituted by Christ the Lord and entrusted to the Church, as they are the actions of Christ and the Church, stand out as the signs and means by which the faith is expressed and strengthened, worship is rendered to God and the sanctification of humankind is effected, and they thus contribute in the highest degree to the establishment, strengthening and manifestation of ecclesial communion.[25]

What was expressed so tersely in 1915 is now expressed in a most lengthy way. The reason for this expansion is, of course, the documentation of Vatican II, and particularly the passages cited above on the Church as a sacrament. One might not be quite satisfied with this description of sacrament, since it does not clearly state that the Church is a sacrament, but it is at least an official effort to come to grips with the broader understanding of sacrament authorized by Vatican II.

One must also consider the official statement in the documents of the Council of Trent, namely, "If anyone says that the sacraments of the new law are not all instituted by our

Lord Jesus Christ, or are more or less than seven, namely, baptism, confirmation, etc., or even that some of these seven are not true and proper sacraments, let that person be anathema" (D. 1601). The bishops at Vatican II had no qualms in calling the Church a sacrament, indeed a universal sacrament. Looked at in a purely numerical way, one could say that there are eight sacraments. Likewise, there has been no anathema thrown to those Catholic theologians who say that Jesus is a sacrament along with the Church as a sacrament. These theologians propound, numerically speaking, nine sacraments. Again, we see that there is a difficulty in interfacing Jesus in his humanity, the Church, and the traditional seven sacraments. It is precisely this issue of interrelating all of these that has caused the renewal of sacramental theology in our times. The interrelationship cannot take place within the popular definition of sacrament, which has dominated sacramental theology in the Catholic Church for so long. A new working definition needs to be established, and until now such a working definition has not been devised. The canon in the new Code, cited above, is indicative of this struggle for a working definition which adequately meets all the issues. Again, let us simply note the problem and postpone the resolution.

3. The Ecumenical Movement

The last hundred years has seen a remarkable development in the ecumenical movement. The seriousness on the part of the Churches to reach some better unity can only be ascribed to the working of the Holy Spirit. Up to the middle of this present twentieth century, it would have been unthinkable to work theologically as far as Catholic theologians were concerned along with Protestant colleagues. The decree of Vatican II on ecumenism, *Unitatis Redintegratio,* officially changes this separatist attitude. Indeed, at the highest level of Roman Catholic administration, there are authorized dialogues with Protestant and with Orthodox theologians. At national episcopal levels in many countries, dialogues have been authorized. From these many dialogues throughout the Christian world, statements have been formulated and many of these deal with the sacraments. One has only to consider the so-called *Lima Document* of the World Council of Churches, *Baptism, Eucharist and Ministry*,[26] to note the focus on sacramental theology. One could also consider the topics discussed in the Lutheran-Catholic dialogues of the United States, which deal with baptism, Eucharist and ministry. The Anglican/Roman Catholic dialogues, sponsored by the Congregation for the Promotion of Christian Unity, and the Lambeth Council deal with Eucharist, ministry and marriage. The same Catholic congregation has issued several documents dealing with the admission of other Christians (Protestants) to Eucharistic Communion in the Catholic Church. In the decree on ecumenism it is noted that the orthodox Churches, though separated from Rome, possess true sacraments (n. 15). In the decree on the Catholic Eastern Churches it is clearly stated that with penance, Eucharist and anointing of the sick a full *communicatio in sacris* is allowable if serious need warrants it, and this with separated Eastern Churches (nn. 26–29).

The history of each of the sacraments described above has aided considerably in these documents between the Churches. One is far more circumspect in making statements on the tradition behind each of the sacraments, and it is because of this history that the various Churches are better able to agree on sacramental theology.

The new emphasis on Church as sacrament and on the humanity of Jesus as sacrament is just beginning to make itself felt in the ecumenical discussion. First of all, the struggle for a new working definition of sacrament is helpful, since the involvement in the definition of the Church itself as a sacrament and especially of Jesus as the primordial sacrament helps to bind together word and sacrament in a way which Protestantism can find more acceptable. With Jesus as the primordial sacrament, the dominance of the word is evident.

On a practical, liturgical basis, the renewal not only of the Catholic ritual, but also of the Book of Common Prayer for the Episcopal Church and of the ritual for a number of major Lutheran synods in the United States has not been done without a great deal of mutual assistance and consultation, even on an official level. It is remarkable that the celebrations of the Eucharist, for instance, in the Catholic, Episcopal and Lutheran Churches are so similar. At times, it might even seem to be identical with certain small areas of liturgical creativity involved. Such similarity has been promoted deliberately by all three Churches.

We note, then, that both in theology and in practice the ecumenical factor has contributed substantially to the renewal of sacramental theology, not only in the Catholic Church, which is our focus, but also in the Episcopal and Lutheran Churches. A step has been taken by Vatican II in its decree on ecumenism which cannot be set to one side. From now on sacramental theology in the Catholic Church can only be done on the basis of ecumenism.

4. Liberation Theology

In the entire Catholic world, liberation theology has made its mark. The Congregation for the Doctrine of the Faith on two occasions, August 6, 1984 and March 22, 1986, published an instruction on the matter.[27] Pope John Paul II has spoken of liberation theology on a number of occasions. CELAM has taken up the topic. In the United States books on liberation theology have been very popular. Whatever one's judgment on liberation theology might be, it has focused considerable attention on itself during the last decade.

As far as sacramental theology is concerned, liberation theology has not addressed itself in any remarkable way to the issue. Even J. Segundo's volume, *The Sacraments Today*,[28] is more a book on the Church than on the sacraments. Nonetheless, liberation theology has concentrated Catholic attention on the social dimension of the Gospel, and this social awareness has indeed affected the way in which one considers the sacraments. Perhaps the liberation theologians have begun in the correct area by presenting the Catholic world with major works on Christology: namely, J. Sobrino's *Cristología desde américa latina (esbozo a partir del seguimiento del Jesús histórico)*,[29] his *Jesus en América Latina*,[30] and L. Boff's *Jesucristo y la Liberación del Hombre*.[31] As mentioned at the start of this chapter, Christological presuppositions shape ecclesiological presuppositions which again shape the sacramental theology. With major works in Christology, the liberation theologians are establishing the basis for more detailed sacramental theology down the line.

Nonetheless, at least indirectly the emphasis on liberation theology has highlighted the social dimension needed for sacramental theology. Sacraments such as penance and to some degree Eucharist as well as anointing of the sick had become quite privatized. The new rites have opened up the social dimension of these sacraments, but liberation theology has accelerated the discussion on this social dimension.

Other factors indeed enter into the renewal of sacramental theology today, and some of these additional factors play a prominent role in individual sacraments. For instance, phenomenology plays a major role in contemporary Eucharistic theology, and to a lesser degree in sacramental theology generally. What we have considered in this chapter have been some of the major factors at work today. The challenge to the traditional definition of sacrament has been noted. With all of this material in mind, let us look in greater intensity at various aspects of sacramental theology.

5. Summary

We can summarize this chapter in the following way:

1. In the last hundred years there has been a great deal of research into the history of each of the sacraments. This history has given us a new appreciation of the sacraments and has renewed the sacramental theology of our time.

2. Just before Vatican II scholars were talking about Jesus as the fundamental sacrament and the Church as a basic sacrament. Vatican Council II officially used the idea of the Church as a basic sacrament. These ideas have expanded the notion of sacrament as used in theology.

3. The ecumenical movement has contributed to the renewal of sacramental theology, especially the ecumenical discussions on baptism, Eucharist and ministry.

4. The highly popular liberation theology, although not directly focused on the sacraments, has emphasized the social dimension of the sacraments. Sacraments should not be seen as privatized acts of prayer.

5. All of these factors, and others as well, have produced a renewal of sacramental theology. In many ways this renewal is somewhat revolutionary, since the popular definition of sacrament is radically challenged, and the Scholastic understanding of sacraments has been opened to the historical and ecumenical dimensions of sacramental thought.

Discussion Questions

1. How does history open up new ways of thinking? What does this mean when applied to sacramental theology?
2. What does "ecumenical" mean? What does the "ecumenical movement" mean? Does this mean our Catholic Church will change?
3. When someone says that the Church itself is a sacra-

ment, what are your first thoughts? How can the Church itself be a sacrament?

4. What is liberation theology? Has the Church approved it? Is a social dimension necessary to Christian faith and theology?

Chapter Two

The Naming and Function of Sacrament

IN THIS CHAPTER WE WANT TO CONSIDER THE VERY NAME *sacrament* and the dynamism behind the notion of sacrament. In all of the Christian Churches of the West, the term sacrament is fairly self-evident, even among those few Protestant groups which prefer to use the term "ordinance." The term sacrament needs no definition; Christians simply know what it means. In the Eastern Churches there is a different term for sacraments—the mysteries—but even among the Eastern Christians the Western term "sacrament" is clear. Let us consider, for a moment, how this situation came to be.

1. The Naming of Sacrament

Jesus never used the term *sacrament,* nor did any of those who wrote parts of the New Testament. Nowhere in any of the New Testament writings is the term sacrament used. Evidently, this name *sacrament* does not come from Jesus nor from the New Testament. Even if we look at the Greek term, *mystery,* we do not find it referring to baptism or Eucharist. In Ephesians we read in the context of a discussion on marriage: "This mystery has many implications" (Eph 5:32). Nonetheless, biblical scholars now refer the term "mystery" to the passage in Genesis, "For this reason a man must leave his father and mother and be joined to his wife; and the two will become one body" (Gen 2:24), rather than to Christian marriage. The passage in Genesis is a "mystery" because it—the passage—has many implications or meanings.[1]

In the New Testament we read about baptism and about the breaking of the bread, but there is no generalized term for these two Christian rituals. The term "baptism" is used quite frequently, as is also a verb form "to baptize." As regards the Eucharist, Paul in 1 Corinthians 11:20 names it the Lord's Supper. In the account of the Supper on the night before Jesus died, Paul uses the verb: "to give thanks" (Eucharist). We find the same use of the verb in Luke, Mark and Matthew, as they recount the meal which Jesus had with his disciples prior to his death (Lk 22:17, 19; Mk 14:23; Mt 26:27). "Eucharist" came to be one of the more prominent terms to refer to this Christian ritual. But at this early date there was no overarching term, such as sacrament, which might refer to *both* baptism and Eucharist.

The same conclusion is evident when we consider the documents on both baptism and Eucharist in the early Church up to 200 A.D. Such documents as the *Didache,* the letters of St. Ignatius of Antioch, the *Apology* of Justin, the *Epitaph* of Abercius and the *Apostolic Tradition* of Hippolytus refer to baptism and to Eucharist, but once more there is no generalized term for these, such as "sacrament." In 150 and thereafter, when a reconciliation rite can also be verified, this reconciliation rite, together with baptism and Eucharist, are not called "sacraments."

The earliest Christian documents were written in Greek, and since *sacramentum* is a Latin term it naturally will not be found in the Greek material. Some theologians, however, simply note that the Greek term for "sacrament" is *mysterion,* but the situation is far more complex. First of all, the Greek word *mysterion* has a long history in Greek culture, antedating by centuries Christian theology. In this Greek history, *mysterion* was used as a religious term. Its root meaning, to close one's mouth or one's lips, fits in well with

religious mystery cults, in which the presence of the divine
overawed the participants and in front of the holy they did
indeed close their lips. Cults grew up in the Greek world
which were called "mystery cults," because of their special
theophanies. Plato used the term mystery in his writings,
and in family life mystery came to mean a secret. When
Christians began to use this term, they often applied it to the
"false cults" of the Gnostics, and when they used it for Christian realities, mystery took on a wide reference: Ignatius
calls the virginity of Mary a mystery (Eph 19:1); Justin calls
the Old Testament covenant a mystery (Dial. 44); Origen
considers the threefold appearance of the Logos (in the incarnation, in the Church, and in the Scriptures) a mystery.[2]

The manner in which the term mystery came to be applied
to the Christian rituals of baptism, Eucharist, etc., is not totally clear from an historical standpoint. Such an attribution
of mystery to the rituals came, in the Greek-speaking world,
at a later date than the first three centuries of the Christian
Church. In other words, the Greek world did not have an
overarching term for what we today call sacraments.

In the West, this was not the case. Tertullian (d. circa 220)
seems to be the first Latin writer to use the term *sacramentum* in a theological way. An early Latin translation of the
Bible used in the North African Church did translate the
Greek *mysterion* by *sacramentum*. This would have given
Tertullian a base for his usage. Tertullian uses the term *sacramentum* for many elements of the Christian faith—for the
Trinity, and for the saving work of God in history—but it is
his use of *sacramentum* for baptism and Eucharist which has
proved to be so influential. In baptism and in the Eucharist,
Tertullian saw the mysterious presence of God, and so the
connection *mysterion/sacramentum* plays no small role. For
baptism, Tertullian adds the Latin meaning of the term *sacramentum*, namely, an oath of allegiance, which corresponds to the baptismal promise. One must clearly note,
however, that Tertullian in no way has a *sacramental theology*, that is, a doctrine on baptism and Eucharist which he

refers to as sacramental theology. Tertullian simply uses the term *sacrament* for both baptism and Eucharist. This same manner of speaking was continued by Cyprian, also of North Africa, with no significant change.[3]

It is only when we come to Augustine (354–430) that we find a true sacramental theology, even though this sacramental theology involves *only* baptism and Eucharist. It is Augustine who speaks of a sacrament as a *sacrum signum* or a *verbum visibile* (a sacred sign or visible word). For Augustine, a step is taken in which sacrament is rooted in its sign character.[4]

Augustine employs the term *sacrament* for many things, not just baptism and Eucharist, but he does so on the basis of this sign character. For Augustine, there is a hidden, mysterious reality which enters into our human world through special signs. The distinction between the reality and the sign is the basis of a true sacramental theology. It is this combination of reality/sign which will be developed in a very rigorous way after 1000, but we can say that after Augustine, roughly after 400 A.D., two issues are very important for the Western world of theology and liturgical practice:

1. The word *sacramentum,* first put forward by Tertullian, grows in theological acceptability throughout the West, until it becomes a technical theological term for the Christian rituals, at first baptism and Eucharist, and then the other rituals as well.

2. The word *sacramentum* is further specified as to its sign character, so that the Western theological world began (slowly at first) to develop a theology of sacrament around the relationship of reality/sign.

Isidore of Seville (d. 633) stressed the remembrance aspect of the sacramental ritual, and although he did this in a very rudimentary way, his teaching influenced the theologians after 1000 in a quite dramatic way, so that the sacraments themselves recalled the saving activity of God in the incarnation.[5]

The use of the name *sacrament* is, then, of a late date, and in no way goes back either to Jesus or to the New Testament generally. Besides the name, one must also say that there was until Augustine, and then only in a very beginning sort of way, *no overarching name or theory* for sacraments. In other words, one did not start with either a generic name, *sacrament,* nor a generic theory, *sacramental theology,* and then develop an understanding of baptism, Eucharist, etc. Rather, one started with the individual rites, baptism, Eucharist, and only in the most gradual way did a unifying "theology of sacraments" develop. Indeed, we can only speak of this kind of unifying theology after 1000 A.D. This tells us that the definition of sacrament is not the most important item, but rather the actual celebration of such rituals as baptism, Eucharist, etc.

A realization of this naming process helps us today in our ecumenical discussions, since a sacramental theology based on seven sacraments causes a number of problems between the various Christian Churches. An historically nuanced approach to this seven-sacrament theology program cannot but help the dialogue between the Churches. Moreover, a definition of sacrament based on an overarching understanding of the various rites, namely, the definition which has become so standard, a sacred sign, instituted by Christ to give grace, is seen as a result of this naming process, not a beginning. In other words, the definition did not determine what is or what is not a sacrament; rather, the Christian community's rituals gave rise to such a definition. This popular and standard definition of sacrament, it should be recalled, was used by both Catholic and Protestant theologians at the time of the Reformation. Both sides maintained that a sacrament was an outward sign instituted by Christ to give grace. Not the definition, but only the extent of the definition, became a matter of dispute.

The history of the naming and the theology which arises

from it puts into perspective, historically, such a definition. In contemporary theology, in which Jesus in his humanity and the Church itself are seen as sacraments, a "redefinition" of sacrament is seen as not only desirable but also as possible. The standard definition of sacrament, hallowed as it is in the Christian tradition, does not go back to Jesus or to the early Church, and must therefore be seen as time-conditioned. In the first chapter we mentioned on several occasions the contemporary problem of the standard definition, and this history of the naming of sacrament helps us one step further toward a possible resolution.

2. The Dynamism Behind the Notion of Sacrament

Augustine's emphasis on the sign character of a sacrament has been a matter of study for centuries after him. Sacraments are in the general category of signs: not all signs are sacraments, Scholastic theologians note, but all sacraments are signs. One could also use the term *symbol.* Symbols, too, are in the general category of sign, and once again all symbols are signs, but not all signs are symbols. Sometimes, however, the limits of sign and symbol become quite disputed.

John Macquarrie and Edward Robinson, in a footnote to their translation of Heidegger's *Being and Time,* attempt a lengthy footnote to clarify some of Heidegger's thought. When one speaks of an appearance, one notes, they write, the following distinct elements:[6]

  1. An observable event, *y,* such as a symptom which announces a disease, *x,* by showing itself, and in and through which *x* announces itself without showing itself.
  2. There is *y*'s showing itself.
  3. There is *x*'s announcing itself in or through *y.*
  4. There is the mere appearance, *y* which *x* may bring

forth when *x* is such a kind that its real nature can *never* be made manifest.

   5. There is the mere appearance which is the *bringing forth* of a mere appearance as noted above in n. 4.

   This may sound highly abstract, but it tells us something of great importance about signs. Macquarrie and Robinson use the case of illness and its symptoms. A symptom announces a disease. We do not see the disease; we see only the symptom (n. 1). The symptom itself is a manifest event (n. 2). The disease, however, is manifest, but only through the symptom (n. 3). In some cases the only way in which we know about a disease is in and through the symptoms; the disease can never manifest itself directly (n. 4—certain mental problems, for example). In these cases the symptom is making manifest or bringing forth the presence of the disease. Heidegger is dealing with the relationship between sign and reality: the symptom is the sign, and the disease is the reality. The most important aspect, for sacraments, in the five points above is the fourth: namely, a reality can be made manifest *only through a sign*. Were one to remove the sign, then the reality could not be made manifest at all. It is precisely this kind of relationship which we are discussing in sacramental sign and sacramental reality. In everyday life, this occurs again and again, particularly in the area of human affection. Love is a reality which can only be made manifest through signs, such as kissing and embracing, and even sexuality. The recurrence of these signs is necessary to maintain the manifestation of the reality of love.

   When the relationship between reality and sign is of such a nature that the reality cannot be made manifest except in and through a sign, then we have a dynamism which is at work in the sacraments. I do not want to give the impression that this situation could not have been otherwise; God could have worked out our salvation without baptism and Eucharist. To use a Scotistic dictum, *de potentia Dei absoluta,* this is quite possible. However, on the basis of revelation, as we find it in the New Testament, baptism and Eucharist, *de potentia Dei ordinata,* are the ways in which God has chosen to bring about our salvation.[7] Thus, the relationship is present, not because of any intrinsic necessity, but because of God's own will. In this we see that fundamentally sacraments must be seen in the light of God's grace, i.e., a gift of God, not a necessary human situation.

The sign, itself, however is a phenomenon, and again to cite Heidegger, a phenomenon generally has a part of its reality which proximately and for the most part does not reveal itself. Hence, signs are of themselves ambiguous, in the French understanding of *ambiguité,* polyvalent. Depending on the way in which the sign itself reveals itself, can one begin to see not only the sign value (n. 2 above) but also the reference (n. 5 above). If we see things in this way, we understand better that baptism, for instance, has a polyvalent sign value, referring to several aspects of the divine reality. At one occasion in history, certain aspects are emphasized over others. This is what is happening today when we begin to see the Church as a sacrament. This was not common currency in theology prior to Vatican II, but now has official endorsement. In other words the sign *sacrament* was until now proximately and for the most part hidden. A certain newness of the sign-sacrament has come to light, and we are seeing a valency of "sacrament" which we never noted before, namely, that the Church itself is a sacrament. The same is true as regards Jesus in his humanity as the fundamental sacrament. This situation, too, was not theologically part of the Christian scene until most recently. What was proximately and for the most part as regards the sign hidden has emerged, and once again the valency of the sign has changed, so that Jesus in his humanity is perceived as the fundamental sacrament.[8]

The use of Heidegger is meant only as a help. I do not mean to canonize Heidegger's approach, but unless something quite similar to Heidegger's analysis of sign is employed, it would be difficult to see how in the twentieth century, and only then, could a Christian theologian come to understand Jesus in his humanity and the Church as a sacrament. It would also be impossible, if one did not have some sort of dynamic understanding of sign/reality as noted above, to explain why there could emerge a seven-sacrament theology only in the twelfth century. The dynamism of the notion of sacrament is caught up in this kind of polyvalency between reality on the one hand, and sign on the other, as well as in the very concept of sign itself.

However, this leads us to an implication of this dynamism which needs to be further appreciated.

3. The Principle of Sacramentality

To speak of the principle of sacramentality is, perhaps, a different way of approaching the question of the sacraments, but nonetheless it is helpful to look at sacramentality in this way.[9] Tillich makes a distinction between a concept or essence and a principle; he writes:

> A concept is dynamic which has within itself the possibility to render understandable the new and unanticipated realizations of some historical provenance. Such concepts I wish to call principles. A principle contains not the abstract-universal of a large number of individual phenomena, but it possesses the real possibility, the dynamism, the power of an historical reality. A principle can never be simply abstracted out of the collectivity of its individual actualizations, for the principle stands critically and judgementally over against its actualization and is not merely the factor which grounds and sustains it. There can be no opposition between essences and their realization. To arrive at a principle is possible in no other way than through an understanding which always involves a decision.[10]

Tillich mentions that an essence is one thing, a principle is quite different. An essence is realized totally in all of its manifestations, e.g., every human being, no matter how young or how old, no matter how ill or how healthy, no matter how intelligent or how retarded intellectually, is a human, and must be treated as such. A principle, however, is quite different. There is, for instance, a principle of justice, which operates, one hopes, in all halls of justice. On the other hand, the principle of justice criticizes each court proceeding, since no one single court proceeding exemplifies to the full the complete meaning of justice. Again, there is a principle of government which we find operative in every governmental structure. However, the principle of government stands over and against each and every manifestation of government since no governmental structure expresses fully what the principle of government is all about.

This same pattern holds true as regards the sacraments. In essence, all baptisms can be considered equal. It is on this basis of essentiality that the ecumenical movement has made such great strides, mutually recognizing the baptisms celebrated in the various Churches. As a principle, however, the principle of baptismal sacramentality stands over and against, i.e., criticizes, each and every actual baptism in each and every Christian Church, not because essentially a baptism is improper, but because the actual baptizing does not reflect what baptism as a sacrament in all its polyvalency is about. One is baptized, for instance, into the Catholic Christian community, into an Anglican Christian community, or into the Lutheran Christian community. Mutually, each Church recognizes the baptism of the other. Still, the division of Christianity falls under the critique of the principle of baptismal sacramentality.

The same can be said of the Eucharist. The essence of each Eucharist is, indeed, preserved, and it is this essence which again allows for agreement among the Churches on Eucharistic theology. But each Eucharist is celebrated in its denominational separation, and so the principle of Eucharistic sacramentality criticizes the actual Eucharist, insofar as that Eucharist does not recognize the unity of all Christians.

The same can be said of the Church as a sacrament. Essentially, the Church is found, as Vatican II says, in the Roman Catholic community, but the principle of ecclesial sacramentality criticizes each manifestation of Church, since it does not reflect what the total and undivided Christian Church is all about.

This principle must not be considered only from the negative side, however, since it is the principle which stirs the continual purification of each and every aspect of ecclesial life, whether that be of an individual sacrament or of the Church as a total community. The principle of sacramentality is a positive way of expressing what has been called the "protestant principle"—i.e., a principle of continuous reformation. The principle of sacramentality is a power in the symbol. To cite Tillich once more, "A principle is authority."[11] It authors and gives origination to the specific entity involved. It is the structuring force within an entity which gives the being identity and consistency, developmental possibilities and creative actuation. "It is this structuring force which in large part gives to a symbol its own power, and the more powerful symbols have incarnated within themselves more of this power of principle, while the less powerful symbols are deficient in such structuring forces."[12]

If the sacraments were simply static, then all the Christian communities would be doing is repeating over and over again a ritualized rote. If, however, the sacraments are dynamic, then one must consider those factors which make up the dynamism, and particularly the dynamism of sign.

4. Summary

We can summarize this chapter as follows:

1. Jesus did not call baptism or Eucharist "sacraments."
2. The New Testament nowhere calls baptism and Eucharist "sacraments."
3. The early Church did not have a name for sacraments, either in the East or in the West.

4. In the Greek-speaking world the term *mysterion* was used for many sacred realities in the Christian community. It is not until the age of Justinian that we see *mysterion* used in any sustained way as a technical term for the "sacraments."

5. In the West, Tertullian seems to be the first author to describe baptism and Eucharist as sacraments, but he did not have any general theology of sacrament. St. Cyprian, who followed him in North Africa, simply continued Tertullian's usage.

6. It was Augustine who first began to develop a theology of sacraments, with his analysis of a sacred sign. After Augustine, Isidore of Seville began to emphasize the idea of remembrance.

7. One can speak meaningfully of a seven sacrament theology only after 1100. Between Augustine and 1100 a gradual development in a sacramental theology emerged in the West.

8. The sign aspect of sacraments involves one in a dynamism of sacrament and sign. This dynamism focuses on the relationship between reality and sign.

9. The reality in the sacraments, because of God's gracious will, can only be made manifest in and through the sign. In other words, the sign is needed to make present the reality of God's love in this particular way.

10. This dynamism involves a principle of sacramentality. The principle of sacramentality stands over and against any and all manifestations of the sacrament. This is its negative aspect.

11. The positive aspect of the principle of sacramentality is its power inherent in the sign to make the polyvalent nature of the sign ever more and more clarified.

1. What does "mystery" mean? Why is this a good name for the sacraments?
2. In the brief survey on the history of the name "sacrament" what was the most striking issue you noted? Why was this important to you?
3. Explain in your own terms what the dynamism of a sacrament is all about.
4. Explain in your own terms what the principle of sacramentality is all about.

Chapter Three

Methodology and the Christian Sacraments

METHODOLOGY HAS ALWAYS PLAYED A MAJOR ROLE IN THE-ology, and in the area of sacraments this is clearly the case. However, one must realize that there is never a single methodology. Rather, there are always several methodologies involved in the study of any part of theology. Such sacraments as baptism and Eucharist are found in the New Testament. Therefore, the methodologies necessary for solid, scholarly biblical exegesis must play a role, not simply to make sure that the text is critically established, but also that the context is critically established. Such methodologies are not the focus of this chapter.

Secondly, historical studies have their own methodologies, which must be honored when doing any kind of historical research. As mentioned in Chapter One, historical research on the sacraments has contributed in no small measure to the renewal of the sacraments. Again there are textual methodologies and hermeneutical methodologies which play a role in historical research. These, too, are not the focus of this chapter.

Once the biblical material and its interpretation have been established, and once the historical data pertinent to the issue under consideration have been determined, then there are two methods which are brought into play to understand the sacraments. These two methods are the focus of the chapter and can be considered the methods needed for systematic theology, which builds on the foundations of the biblical and historical data. One of the methods will be called the Christological approach; the other will be referred to as the phenomenological approach. Other names might be substituted, but the material under each heading seems to be crucial for an understanding, theologically, of the sacraments in today's world.[1]

Both methods are needed, for a method is only a means of grasping a specific part of a larger picture, in order to study it, identify it and appraise it. Without the Christological method, the faith aspect of the sacraments would be jeopardized. Without the phenomenological method, the human aspect of the sacraments would be negated. Let us consider each of these in detail.

1. The Christological Approach

In contemporary theology of the sacraments the Christological approach has been profoundly changed. When the popular definition of sacrament held sway, Jesus was only mentioned in the phrase "instituted by Christ," and theologians jostled to find the exact historical moment when Jesus actually instituted this or that sacrament. Jesus reappears, indirectly, in the phrase "to give grace." The grace that is meant here is the grace of Christ, the grace of salvation of the new covenant.

When one speaks about Jesus as the primordial sacrament, a wholly new dimension appears. Jesus is the very reason why anything in the new covenant might be called and be in fact a sacrament. Jesus is in this view not simply another sacrament beyond the other seven, but Jesus is the primordial sacrament, the very reason for sacramentality. The same type of reasoning lies behind the theological understanding of the Church as a sacrament. The Church is not simply another sacrament alongside seven others, but the Church is a basic or foundational sacrament. The Church, too, is the reason why baptism, Eucharist, etc., can even be called and be in fact a sacrament. One can see immediately that the Christological and the ecclesiological elements in an understanding of sacrament are, today, crucial. For this reason the Christological method is of tantamount importance.

In the case of Jesus as primordial sacrament, there are a number of issues which must be considered:

(a) Jesus in his humanity is the basis for Jesus as primordial sacrament. This is not stressed enough, even by such theologians as K. Rahner and Schillebeeckx. We have spoken above that a sacrament involves a relationship between sign and reality. The sign is *not* the reality, nor is it of the same value as the reality. If one is in direct contact with a reality, no signs are needed; in this respect, the signs are seen as secondary, dependent, relativized. The reality is the superior part of this relationship. Consider, for a moment, using this reality/sign relationship within the Trinity itself. In this instance God the Father is the reality, God the Son would be the sign (so close to the image of God, Logos of the Father, descriptions). But if the sign is secondary, dependent, relativized vis-à-vis the reality, then only God the Father is really God. The Son is "less than God" and we are back to Arianism and subordinationism, heresies which the Church rejected after centuries of struggle. The divine nature of Jesus must not be part of this primordial sacramentality of Jesus. R. Schulte has written many fine things on the sacraments, but the following statement, similar in many ways to things K. Rahner and Schillebeeckx say, does not seem to be correct:

> If Jesus Christ is to be described as the original sacrament (Ur-Sakrament) of our salvation, the thinking here is focused actually on him personally, on his person, uniting the divine and

human nature, in the understanding of the hypostatic union elsewhere discussed and in his work of salvation for us.[2]

The person of Jesus is the divine person, the second person of the Trinity, and therefore God. The basis of his sacramentality is not specifically in his human nature, but in his divine person. We are clearly flirting with a dangerous understanding of Trinity, in which the second person, ultimately, is the original sacrament. Far better, it seems to me, is to state categorically from the first that Jesus in his human nature *alone* is the original sacrament.

(b) The sign aspect of sacrament needs to be something perceptible, and this clearly is Jesus' human nature. As 1 John expresses it: "What we have heard and we have seen with our own eyes, what we have watched and touched with our hands" (1 Jn 1:1).

This perceptible aspect of Jesus we find not in his divinity nor in his risen humanity, but in his earthly humanity. One returns to the Gospels, to the portrait of Jesus in Palestine, to see the perceptible aspect of Jesus as sacrament. One proceeds from Jesus to the Church to the individual sacramental rite. The starting point is the humanity of Jesus.

Already Vatican II pointed us in this direction. In the decree on the ministry and life of priests, *Presbyterorum Ordinis,* the bishops begin their reflections with Jesus, in his humanity as priest: "The Lord Jesus, 'whom the Father consecrated and sent into the world' (Jn 10:36)" (n. 2). As God the Father does not consecrate the second person of the Trinity nor send him into the world, the bishops are focusing on the humanity of Jesus, consecrated and sent as priest into the world. From there the text moves to the Church. Jesus "makes his whole mystical body sharer in the anointing of the Spirit wherewith he has been anointed, for in that body all the faithful are made a holy and kingly priesthood, they offer spiritual sacrifices to God through Jesus Christ, and they proclaim the virtues of him who has called them out of darkness into his admirable light" (n. 2).

Only after this Christ-to-Church movement do the bishops take up the ordained ministry: "However, the Lord also appointed certain men as ministers, in order that they might be united in one body in which 'all the members have not the same function' (Rom 12:4). These men were to hold in the community of the faithful the sacred power of order" (n. 2).

We find the same Christological approach in the introduction, *Praenotanda,* of the decree on the renewal of the sacrament of reconciliation. The body of the decree opens with a description of the mystery of reconciliation in Jesus:

> The Father has shown forth his mercy by reconciling the world to himself in Christ and by making peace for all things on earth and in heaven by the blood of Christ on the cross. The Son of God made man lived among men in order to free them from the slavery of sin and to call them out of darkness into his wonderful light. He therefore began his work on earth by preaching repentance and saying: "Turn away from sin and believe the good news" (Mk 1:15).[3]

The decree goes on to state that Jesus not only preached reconciliation, but welcomed sinners and healed the sick. Finally, he even died on the cross for our sins and rose from the dead to justify us. He preached and lived reconciliation. All of this section is focused on the humanity of Jesus: his words, his actions, his death, his rising from the dead.

Once this has taken place, the decree turns to the Church as a locus of reconciliation. In this small—three paragraphs—section (nn. 3–5) the Church is presented as a community which has sinners within, but also as a community which always is in need of purification. The Church shares in the sufferings of Jesus, undergoing difficulties and trials. The Church is a sign to the world of conversion to God. There is, in the Church, a continuous process of reconciliation. The emphasis here is on those visible situations in which the Church and the members of the Church give evidence in their actions and lives of God's grace of reconciliation.

Only against this background does the decree then turn to

the sacrament of reconciliation, which is the main focus of
the decree and the renewed rite of penance which follows this
introduction.

One could look at almost all of the new rites, baptism,
anointing, confirmation, etc., and see that a definite emphasis has been taken to highlight the role of Jesus, first
of all, and then the Church in the sacramental activity.
What we have alluded to here is clear enough: the structure
of this approach is: Jesus—Church—the individual sacrament. What the official Church documents allude to in this
approach is a model for us in our own attempt to understand the meaning of the sacraments. Begin with Jesus,
then go to the Church, and *only* then discuss the individual
sacrament.

2. The Phenomenological Approach

As early as 1949, the Dutch Protestant theologian, G. van
der Leeuw, in his book *Sakramentstheologie,* noted that the
sacraments in the Christian tradition had become a sort of
"epiphenomenon" to human life.[4] They seem to have nothing
directly to do with human life, but come "from above" as a
sort of extra dimension. Indeed, van der Leeuw complains,
sacraments have been discussed as strictly Christian enti-
ties, as though there were no sacraments among other religious groups and other cultures. Rather, he wants to
emphasize, sacraments are anchored deep in the human
structures. It is this relationship to the human structures of
life that we call a phenomenological approach, since sacraments respond to the phenomenon of being human. The
Catholic Church has already experienced this change in the
various texts or study guides developed recently for the
teaching of sacraments in our multi-leveled school situations. The long-standing *Baltimore Catechism* paid little attention to the human aspects of the sacraments. The answers

in the catechism focused almost exclusively on the divine or revealed aspect: What is a sacrament? How many are there? From whom do the sacraments receive their power to give grace? Do the sacraments give sanctifying grace? Do each of the sacraments also give a special grace? Do the sacraments always give grace?[5] Even in dealing with the individual sacraments there is little room for the human structures and substrate. Baptism deals with original sin, the character, the minister, the form, the necessity of baptism for all, baptism of desire, the role of godparents, the need to baptize infants after birth. Nowhere is there any mention that baptism is rooted in the human as well as in the divine. Baptism is seen clearly as an "epiphenomenon," a phenomenon on top of (*epi*) the human phenomenon: grace builds on nature.

Today, such an approach is seen as pedagogically unsound. It is also theologically unsound. The incarnation is based on the entry of the divine into the human, not on the divine as an epiphenomenon of the human. Consequently, we have today a sort of "unpacking" of the human dimension to see how each sacrament helps perfect human life. Already Pius XII in *Mystici Corporis* indicated in a brief way that the sacraments accompany human life from birth to death and take place at important moments of human life.[6] Although this procedure of equating sacramental life to human benchmarks has not been followed, it nonetheless points out the modeling that the official Church was attempting to give, even at mid-century, by way of an impetus into this humanization process.

One of the difficulties of this phenomenological approach has already been alluded to, namely, the polyvalency of the sacramental sign itself. Just as life itself is not simplistic, so, too, sacramental life is not simplistic, and care must be taken to focus on the main aspects of human life which connect well with the sacramental signs. As a first step we need to line up the various sacraments which Vatican II theology has propounded:

Jesus in his humanity
The Church
Baptism/confirmation
Eucharist
Reconciliation
Marriage
Anointing
Orders

We then ask what is the human phenomenon or phenomena which best complement these individual sacramental structures. Let us consider each instance:

1. *Jesus in His Humanity.* What does it mean to be human? There are, of course, many replies to this question, but interpersonal relationship certainly plays a major role in the healthiness of human life. Indeed, if one were to ask the opposite question—When does one feel most inhuman?—the answer more often than not would focus on loneliness, i.e., when there are no interpersonal relationships. One can feel humanly quite fulfilled even if one is in prison or on trial. If one is defending a cause, there is purpose to life. But if there are no more causes, no one who cares about one's own cause, if one is all alone, then the feeling of human waste, human lack, takes over. This flip-side of the coin tells us that being human occurs in a powerful way when there are deep human relationships in one's life. Given this, we then look to the life of Jesus and see that he experienced deep human relationships: with his mother, Mary; with Lazarus, Mary and Martha, whom, we read, he loved; with his disciples, both men and women. We will see Jesus as a sacrament of God's love for us when we begin to understand his human bonding and relationships, with the poor and the rejected, with the disciples and relatives, with friends, and even his attempt to relate to those who turned against him, the priests, the Pharisees, the scribes.

2. *The Church.* Like every society, the Church has a whole array of signs and symbolism—church buildings,

church ritual, church banners, church hierarchy, church pictures which we find in homes and work places. Indeed, there is an abundance of sign and symbolism, and in many ways all of these contribute to the sign character of the Church. Many of these signs in the Church are acculturated, belonging to a Western and a European culture, rather than a different culture. Colors, for instance, have a different meaning in one culture than they do in others, so that liturgical colors do not have universal signification.

However, every culture has community units, and it is this formation of community which seems to lie at the heart of the Church as a sign. All those interpersonal dynamics which bring about a community of men and women form the sign that a community is coming together, and also that the Church is being formed into the people of God. It will surely be the unpacking of those rituals and dynamics and signs in the Church community which will clarify the Church as sacrament. Conversely, elements which indicate disunity will hide the Church as sacrament, even deform it.

3. *Baptism/Confirmation.* These two sacraments are considered together, since originally and historically they are intrinsically bound to each other. The reasons for this unity can be found in the study of both baptism and confirmation. For our purposes we will simply presuppose this unity and search for that human element which undergirds both rituals. Over the years, theologians have tended to see baptism as the sacrament of initiation. Recent study has indicated that the real "sacrament of initiation" is the process of baptism (confirmation), Eucharist. Even the new ritual of the Church bears this out. Baptism and birth, however, have often been compared, but baptism for many centuries was primarily administered to adults, not infants, and in some Protestant Churches this is still the rule. The Catholic ritual, the RCIA, would find it difficult to equate birth and baptism, since the RCIA is precisely meant for adults who have already been born and have been living for

some time. The Johannine indication of a "new birth" or a "birth from above" (Jn 3:3–5) provides us with a better clue. Baptism/confirmation is talking about life, and in baptism we celebrate life: both the life that we have through birth and the life that we have in the Spirit. *Life,* therefore, seems to be the key, the human element or phenomenon which helps us to see what total life, including life in the Spirit, is all about. Since we can celebrate life at any stage of human existence, so, too, baptism/confirmation has meaning at any stage of our existence. If this were not so, then a Church would have to baptize either at infancy or at adulthood, but this does not seem to square with Church history and present Church practices.

4. *Eucharist.* The meal aspect of the Eucharist is rooted in the New Testament, and it would seem that this is the dominant or at least one of the dominant factors of Eucharistic celebration. Around the time of Theodore of Mopsuestia (d. 428) there seems to be a de-emphasizing of the meal aspect of the Eucharist, and a major emphasizing of the death/resurrection of Jesus. This led, of course, to the emphasis on Eucharistic sacrifice.[7] Still, it is the meal which contextualizes the New Testament data on the Lord's Supper. As a result, it is the ordinary human meal that offers a central human phenomenon to understand the dynamism of Eucharistic sacramentality.

Present-day Church practice also indicates this. The table of the Lord is the central point in the Church, not the tabernacle. Sharing the Eucharistic food is pivotal in the renewed liturgies of the Mass. Communion is much more emphasized today than adoration of the consecrated bread and wine in such services as benediction, forty hours, etc. It would seem that the official Church is urging us to see the Eucharist as a communal meal in a very centralized way. Therefore, unpacking all those dynamics which contribute to people-eating-together helps us to understand better the meaning of the Eucharist.

5. *Reconciliation*. The renewed rite stresses the name "reconciliation," without, however, abandoning "penance." Still, it seems to be the intention of the official Church to renew this sacrament by a better understanding of reconciliation than through a better understanding of penance. Reconciliation, as is evident, is a major part of human life generally. Human relationships have a way of becoming stronger at times and of becoming strained at other times. Whenever there is a strained relationship, reconciliation is needed. How often do we use the simple phrase "Sorry" in our daily life. How deep this "Sorry" is depends on the intensity of the relationship and the depth of the strain. To reflect on a day of human existence and to note the number of occasions when reconciliation, in one form or another, is needed helps us to understand the dynamics of this sacrament of reconciliation. Moreover, in human reconciliation there are two elements: the active one of reconciling, and the passive one of accepting reconciliation. Both sides are needed to understand the depths of the sacrament of reconciliation. Forgiving our neighbor is part of this sacrament; the experience of the grace of forgiveness by a loving God is also and even more profoundly part of this sacramental event.

6. *Marriage*. Over the long history of this sacrament an argument has taken place as to the "essence" of the sacrament of marriage: Is marriage essentially a contract? Or is it essentially consent? Canon lawyers have tended to favor the notion of contract, and theologians have favored that of consent. To understand the phenomenological aspect of the sacrament of marriage let us consider human consent. There is an entire gamut of degree in human consent: from a simple agreement to go to the movies down to a life-commitment such as we find in marriage, in religious life, and even in other career choices. What are the dynamics of human consent? Why is the consent to go to the movies less engaging of the human person than consent to a career? When one begins to understand the intricacies of human consent, then one be-

gins to see that the sacrament of marriage truly involves human marriage generally, and is not simply some additional quality to human marriage which takes place because one is a member of the Church and has been baptized. It is marriage itself which is sacramentalized. This sacramentalization centers around marriage as a consent between two human beings.

7. *Anointing of the Sick.* One must appreciate the efforts today by the official Church to see this sacrament as an anointing of the sick and not a final preparation for death. There is in every human community, a family, a neighborhood, a culture, concern for those who are ill. The showing of this concern is generally done through touch. When a sick person becomes untouchable, alienation takes place and even healing is hard to attain. An untouchable is shunned by the group, considered outside the group. But a touchable illness is cared for and nourished back to life. There is a powerful human dynamic undergirding touch. There are touches of hatred, touches of indifference and touches of love. That touch can involve so much of the human side of relationship cannot go by unnoticed when one approaches an understanding of the sacrament of anointing. Jesus touched and healed. The Church touches and heals. It is in this touching that we see the sign, a perceptible element, of the sacramental event. Oil, too, is part of this, but oil by itself is not the sign; it is the touching with oil, the touching with medication, i.e., the sign. Nor is this a depersonalized medication; rather, it is the *human* application, the human touching with medication that is the sign. Touching is the phenomenon that needs to be unpacked to see the depths of this sacramental activity.

8. *Orders.* The sacrament of orders has had a long history, and at times power has been emphasized: the power to consecrate and the power to forgive sins. Vatican II has moved away from this emphasis, and focused more on the notion of service. This phenomenon, service, seems to be the key in that it provides the human structure for the sacra-

ment of orders. Service is a multi-dimensional category involved in human relationships. One need only think of the many ways in which the term is used: service stations, civil service, the armed services, service organizations. Vatican II documentation holds up as a model for priestly ministry the service of Jesus himself, who came not to be served but to serve. The washing of the feet by Jesus is a powerful statement on the meaning of ordained ministry. In human life, generally, we find many examples of such "washing of the feet." Parents provide much loving service to their children, spouses to each other, friends to one another. It is these instances of loving human service which help us to understand what sharing in the ministry of Jesus is all about, and to unpack the dynamics of service helps us to see the sacramental sign of orders.[8]

A final methodological issue which helps considerably in interpreting signs, symbols and sacraments is the determination of two questions essentially involved in all symbolic events: namely, *of what* is something a sign, symbol or sacrament, and, secondly, *for whom* is something a sign, symbol or sacrament? These two small questions, *of what* and *for whom,* clarify a number of factors. If we apply this to the sacraments enumerated above, we could say that:

1. Jesus in his humanity as a sacrament is a sign *of* God's forgiving love for all men and women. Jesus is, therefore, a sacrament of God.

2. The Church is a sacrament *of* all that Jesus revealed. The Church is, therefore, a sacrament of Jesus.

3. Baptism/confirmation is a sacrament *of* God's gift of life in all its created dimensions, both natural and supernatural.

4. Eucharist is a sacrament *of* Jesus' fellowship with all his followers, men and women, a fellowship that is saving, reconciling, promising.

5. Reconciliation is a sacrament *of* Jesus' forgiveness to all of his followers.

6. Marriage is a sacrament *of* Jesus' love for the Church, manifest in Christian marriage, and the Church's love for Jesus, also manifest in Christian marriage.

7. Anointing is the sacrament *of* Jesus' love for his followers even when they are sick, a love that is with them down to the end of their lives if necessary.

8. Orders is a sacrament *of* Jesus' continuing ministry of service within his Church.

Similarly, the *for whom* question arises, and I would suggest the following:

1. Jesus in his humanity is a sacrament *for* all men and women, Christian or not. Jesus speaks of God to any and all who might see and hear.

2. The Church is also a sacrament *for* all men and women, Christian and non-Christian alike. This seems to be borne out by the Vatican II constitution on the Church, *Lumen Gentium,* in which the light of the entire world is Jesus, and the Church, when it truly acts as Church, reflects the light of Jesus to all men and women.

3. All the other sacraments are *for* the Christian community only. Baptism is a sacrament for Christians, not a sacrament for non-Christians; Eucharist is a sacrament for the Christian community, not for outsiders. In other words, these sacraments are intracommunal; they are some of the major symbols which form the Christian community. Outside of this community they do not operate as significatory events.

Methods are but means, and can never be placed in some sort of untouchable situation. Methods, therefore, can change. What concerns us, theologically and practically, is the way in which we can begin to unlock the mystery of sacramentality. Hopefully, these methods assist us to move to this mysterious center, in which God and Jesus come to presence in our world.

3. Summary

We can summarize this chapter in the following brief sentences:

1. There are many methods involved in the study of the sacraments; some are biblical, some are historical, some are systematic. It is the latter which this chapter treats.

2. The Christological method begins with Jesus in his humanity as a sacrament and then proceeds to Church as fundamental sacrament, and only then to the individual sacramental rituals.

3. Only Jesus in his humanity is a sacrament; to apply sacramentality to his divinity is toying with subordinationism.

4. Official Church documents have provided us with some instances in which this Christological method is clearly used.

5. The phenomenological method attempts to root the sacraments in human structures, and not simply "add" them to our human life as a sort of epiphenomenon.

6. Each of the sacraments, which we find in Vatican II theology, needs to be clarified as regards that phenomenological aspect of human life which corresponds to the sacramental event.

7. The two questions, *of what* and *for whom,* are very helpful in clarifying the meaning of all signs, symbols and sacraments.

Discussion Questions

1. What is a method? What is the purpose of a method?
2. Explain in your own words what the Christological method is all about. Does this help you to understand sacraments? If so, why? If not, why not?

3. Explain the phenomenological method in your own words. Does this help you to understand sacraments? If so, why? If not, why not?
4. Do you agree with the phenomenological referents to human life detailed in this chapter? Are there others you might prefer?
5. Does the section on *of what* and *for whom* help you to understand sacraments in a better way? If so, why? If not, why not?

Chapter Four

God's Action in the Sacramental Event

IN THE CHRISTIAN TRADITION, SACRAMENTS HAVE BEEN ASSO-
ciated with grace. The Catholic tradition speaks of this as
"sacraments giving grace." In the *Baltimore Catechism* we
read: "Grace is a supernatural gift of God bestowed on us
through the merits of Jesus Christ for our salvation." And in
another chapter: "The sacraments do give sanctifying grace
. . . and always give grace if we receive them with the right
dispositions."[1]

For his part John Calvin says that a sacrament is "a tes-
timony of divine grace toward us, confirmed by an outward
sign, with mutual attestation of our piety toward him." This
definition, he notes, is but a clearer explanation of Augustine's teaching that a sacrament is a "visible sign of a sacred
thing," or "a visible form of an invisible grace."[2]

Luther, too, could be quoted in a way similar to Calvin, but
what is at stake here is not the number of sacraments, two
or seven, but rather the relationship of the sacramental action, the use of some external sign, such as bread and wine,
oil, etc., with accompanying words, such as the sacramental
formulas ("I baptize you . . . " "This is my body . . . ") and the
free conferral of grace by God. One can see that this is the
issue of grace and good works. In other words, the issue,
which became so divisive at the time of the Reformation, was
fundamentally not one of the sacraments, but rather one of

the relationship between grace and good works. This is at the heart of the teaching on justification, for both Protestant and Catholic.

Let us go to the period prior to the Reformation and investigate the ways in which this relationship was discussed by theologians. Since the issue became a major part of the theology of the sacraments at the time of the Scholastics, it is necessary to consider what the major Scholastics said on the question. We find that prior to the Reformation there were three differing trends: (1) that of St. Thomas Aquinas, (2) that of moral causality, (3) and that of occasional causality. Let us consider each of these briefly.

1. The Position of St. Thomas Aquinas

St. Thomas' teaching on the relationship of grace and the sacramental activity has been called *instrumental, efficient causality*. For Thomas the primary, efficient cause of all grace is, of course, God. In the Christian Church we do have sacramental actions, such as baptism and Eucharist. In these sacramental actions, certain material things are employed— in the case of baptism, water, and in the case of Eucharist, bread and wine. Since these are found in the word of God, more precisely the New Testament, they are part of revelation, and cannot be substituted by other material things.

The question arises, however, as to the causal influence of such material things in the sacramental action. Thomas says that they are only instrumental, in the way that sensate things give rise to intelligent thought (cf. *Summa Theologica*, 3, q. 60 a. 5). The same can be said of the words, which Thomas mentions in art. 6 of the same question. Material things might have many significations; the words specify the significance, e.g., "This is my body." Both matter and word, then, are instrumental.

Changes in the material things or the words, according to Thomas, might very well go against the intention of Jesus himself, and therefore invalidate the sacramental action (a. 8). Acceptable material things and acceptable words play a role; unacceptable material things and unacceptable words invalidate the sacramental event. What role do these acceptable things and words play in the sacramental event?

The Dominican scholar, Cándido Aniz, in the Spanish translation of the *Summa Theologica* of St. Thomas, stops the text at this juncture and inserts a fourteen page introduction to the question of the causality of the sacraments according to St. Thomas.[3] He notes that a wide variety of opinions have been proposed to describe the genuine thought of St. Thomas. Some authors, he writes, defend an intentional causality; others advocate a moral causality or an instrumental efficient causality. "The question cannot be resolved with noonday clarity, given the fact that the texts of the Angelic Doctor are not conclusive in the way we might wish. There is room for free discussion."[4]

The major reason for this unclarity is that Thomas dealt with the issue on several occasions during his long years of writing: namely, in his *Commentary on the Sentences* (4 d. 1, q. 1, a. 4), in the *De Veritate* (q. 27, a. 4), in the *De Potentia* (q. 3, a. 4) and in the *Summa Theologica* (3. q. 62, a. 1). In the *Sentences* there seems to be a description of the sacraments as physical instruments of efficient causality which cooperate dispositively for grace. In *De Veritate* Thomas appears to present a case for efficient instrumental causality. In *De Potentia,* however, he seems to advocate a dispositive cause with no efficient causality involved. In the *Summa* Thomas speaks of perfective instrumental causality, but there is some unclarity on the matter. Aniz, with hesitation, but still with judgment, believes that one could defend the position that Thomas' thought on the causality of the sacraments can be seen as an efficient, instrumental, perfective causality.[5]

An instrumental cause, Thomas notes in the *Summa,* has two actions: on the one hand the instrument depends on the primary agent for the effect attained, as a saw depends on the artisan using it; on the other hand, the instrument has its own (efficient) effect, as a saw cutting through a board. It would seem to be Thomas' thought that if an instrument does not contribute its own causality (the second above) then it cannot be seen as agent of instrumental causality. Applied to the sacraments, the instruments, such as water, bread, wine, words, etc., contribute something of their own to the effect, which in this case is grace. It is in the interfacing of all of these factors that the issue of grace and good works arises.

The fact that Aniz thought it necessary to insert a fairly detailed personal essay on the issue of sacramental causality in St. Thomas indicates two items which are germane to our present concern: (a) the exact thought of St. Thomas is somewhat in doubt; (b) the issue of causality in sacraments must be theologically so central that it merits an *excursus* of the size and importance which Aniz gives it.

There is no doubt that after Thomas, the majority of Thomistic theologians understood or interpreted St. Thomas as advocating instrumental efficient causality of the sacraments. Some will qualify this by saying that it is "perfective"; others will say that it is "dispositive"; still others will maintain that it is "dispositive, intentional."[6] Perhaps we could summarize this approach as follows:

(a) God alone is the primary efficient agent.
(b) The sacramental rite is only an instrumental, secondary agent.
(c) An instrumental agent, however, involves three things:
    (1) The instrument itself must do something under the influence of the primary agent.
    (2) The instrument must also contribute something proper to itself.
    (3) Therefore, in the effect there must be something

which can be attributed to the instrument as cause.

Over the centuries, Thomistic theologians (but also Scotistic) distinguished the sacraments as cause and as sign. Leeming notes: "The sacrament as cause effects grace, but as a sign it produces only knowledge of its effect as a cause."[7] This separation of sign and cause remained quite sacrosanct in Catholic theology on sacramental causality until our present age, in which K. Rahner took issue with this distinction and attempted to reunite sign and cause. We will consider this later on.

2. Moral Causality

Although moral causality did not really find its expression until the time of Melchior Cano, a Dominican who died in 1560, still it has roots in the Scholastics, particularly St. Thomas, prior to the Reformation. In this view, the sacraments are seen as pleading with God to grant grace. Examples such as money amounting to the price of a slave's freedom or a letter to a friend asking for a favor or the verbal intervention of someone pleading a cause—all these have been used to describe the way in which sacraments "cause grace." Vasquez viewed the sacraments as the very intercession of Christ for or the voice of Christ pleading our cause with God. Franzelin expressed much the same view:

A moral cause, in the strict sense, differs from a mere condition without which the effect does not arise, inasmuch as a moral cause has some power, worth, dignity, excellence, which although it does not physically influence and work towards the very being of the effect, nevertheless it presents a reason to the physical cause, because of which he produces the effect. But, on the contrary, in something which is a mere condition, there is no such worth or power; but it is only something connected

with another, in which other is the true causality, which, however, is only exerted in action when the condition is verified.[8]

One notices immediately that the causal action is not so
much on those who receive the sacraments as on God who
alone, here, produces the effect of grace. In this view the dynamism has been reversed, moving from the sacraments to
God, rather than from God through the instrumental efficiency of the sacrament to the persons involved. It would
seem that there is some danger here of semi-Pelagianism, insofar as we must do something (at least plead the cause first),
and only after that, and in a sense because of that pleading,
does God confer grace.

Still in the post-Reformation period, a number of qualified
Catholic theologians have backed this kind of sacramental
causality: de Ledesma, Vasquez, Lessius, Lugo, Tournely,
Franzelin, Pesch, Sasse, Otten and Puig. A list like this of
such notables indicates that there is certainly something
valid in this moral causality.

The Eastern Churches have never treated sacramental
causality in such a philosophical and analytical way as their
Western counterparts, but it is interesting to note that in the
Eastern sacramental liturgies, the forms usually are depre-
cative: "May the Lord grant . . . " The prayer aspect of the
sacraments in these Eastern Churches is very evident, and
the community is indeed asking God to send his grace and
his Spirit on the community as they celebrate the holy mysteries of the sacraments. There is here some affinity to moral
causality.

We can summarize this moral causality as follows:

1. God is the real efficient agent; he alone causes grace.

2. The sacramental rite is similar to a prayer, a pleading
with God to produce grace.

3. The sacramental rite dynamically looks to God rather
than the recipients, whereas in instrumental, efficient causality the dynamism is recipient-oriented.

3. Occasional Causality

Many theologians have espoused some sort of occasional causality, and the roots of this view are also to be found in the period prior to the Reformation. In this view God alone produces grace, and consequently the sacraments, properly speaking, do not produce grace. The sacraments are seen rather as the occasions through which God himself produces grace. Generally, the Franciscan school has been associated with this trend of thought.

Already the Franciscan Alexander of Hales, even prior to St. Thomas, had set the stage for discussing the question on the causality of the sacraments. At the very beginning of his section on sacramental causality he notes: "I answer without prejudice of a better opinion; I speak by giving an opinion, determining nothing, that sacraments are the cause of some effect in the soul."[9] Alexander realizes that there is some unclarity here, and thus he presents his studied opinion, no more. For him sacraments are not mere dispositions, but there is some sort of causality at work *large sumendo* (i.e., taking effective causality in a very broad sense of the term), "for they dispose a person, making one more suitable for the reception of grace, and even more ready to act with infused grace. And so they are causes of grace, not indeed as regards the *esse* of grace, but as regards the *inesse* of grace in a more suitable and conformable way."[10]

The hesitancy of Alexander should be noted, since we are indeed at a crucial issue: the relationship of grace to good works. This hesitancy carries on throughout the period prior to the Council of Trent, and at the Council of Trent the Dominican and Franciscan theologians were not at one on the matter. Nor did the Council of Trent settle the issues dividing these two schools of theological thought, so that even today the question remains a fairly open one.

St. Bonaventure, who was a colleague of St. Thomas at the University of Paris, proceeds in a typical Scholastic manner, drawing up a list of statements, either propounding or contradicting the main question: whether the sacraments effect grace. Once these lengthy lists and reasons have been put forward, Bonaventure gives his own view, and again we see great caution on the matter.[11]

Bonaventure notes that, given human sin and God's own determination of how to free us from sin, the sacraments in our present economy are *sine qua non*. He qualifies this, however, by noting later that the situation is similar to a king who establishes that anyone having a certain object will receive a hundred marks. After the royal decree the thing itself is not changed in any way, but it is now ordained or endowed with a significance it did not have before. Since the object now enjoys this significance, it is said to be effective.[12] Again, he notes that the Lord has bound himself by a certain pact, namely, that he will give grace to someone who receives a sacrament. "The piety of faith," Bonaventure says, "is not against this position, and reason accedes to it."[13] One sees why this form of causality is called "occasional causality," since it is God who has predetermined the occasion, and on such an occasion he alone confers in an efficient way his grace.

Richard of Mediavilla, another Franciscan theologian who died around 1308, holds the same view as Bonaventure: "The sacrament of the New Law is said to cause grace only because by divine institution a divine power always effects grace in those who receive the sacrament worthily."[14]

John Duns Scotus follows this same line of thought, in which the sacraments "cause" grace insofar as God assists them to cause grace, not in any necessary or absolute way, but in virtue of the power God has given to them.[15] Again, it is the empowerment given by God to the occasion, which is the reason one can say that sacraments give grace. Everything, therefore, is occasioned by God, and the gratuity of grace is maintained.

We can summarize this occasional causality as follows:

1. God is the real agent; he and he alone causes grace.

2. The sacramental rite is a sign, i.e., it has a relationship to God's desire to give grace (Bonaventure) and this is due to the prior ordination by God (Scotus).

3. The term "power" as in the "power of the sacrament," is an extended use of the term.

These were the three theories on sacramental causality which were developed within Scholastic theology. Each has its merits and its problems. Each has its proponents in highly respected Catholic theologians. Each theory remains acceptable teaching within the Catholic Church. It is true that the Thomistic approach of instrumental efficient causality enjoyed a definite "edge" insofar as many of the theology manuals written before Vatican II preferred the Thomistic approach, but the official magisterium has not determined the matter.

H. Jedin, who in our present century has done so much solid research on the history of the Council of Trent, cites a study by D. Iturrioz, "La definicion del Concilio de Trento sobre la causalidad de los sacramentos," in which the author argues that canon 8 of the canons on the sacraments generally does not decide the issue on sacramental causality in favor of the Thomistic position. Jedin, along with many other scholars, concurs in this judgment.[16] The Council of Trent did not settle this matter. After the Council of Trent, Catholic theologians tended to elaborate on one or other of these three views, but in the main did not advance Catholic teaching on the causality of the sacraments in any significantly different way. One of the main reasons for this lack of innovative thought centered around a position which became almost untouchable: the sacraments as causes were one thing; the sacraments as signs were quite another. In other words, sign and cause were kept in a deliberate fashion, quite apart from one another: what was said about sacramental cause did not influence what was said about sacramental sign.

4. Contemporary Catholic Thought on Sacramental Causality

Sacramental causality has not been a major focus of contemporary Catholic theology, but some steps forward have, indeed, been taken. Karl Rahner, once again, has taken the lead on this issue and in his book, *The Church and the Sacraments,* he has readdressed the issue of sacramental causality, and perhaps he has aided us immensely to move forward on the issue. He writes:

> In all these theories it is noteworthy that the fact that the sacraments are signs plays no part in explaining their causality. Their function as signs and their function as causes are juxtaposed without connection. The axiom everywhere quoted, *sacramenta significando efficiunt gratiam* (sacraments effect grace by signifying), is not in fact taken seriously. Nor do these theories take into account the fundamentally human element in the sacraments as sacred rites which have a past and a background in the whole history of man's religious activity. Always and everywhere men have had the conviction that in gestures and rites and figurative representation, what is signified and pointed to is in fact present, precisely because it is "represented," and this conviction should not be rejected off-hand as "analogy magic."[17]

Rahner's main protest revolves around the power of symbolism, and what this power has meant within the history of human life and religious ritual. Such a power has a role to play in the sphere of the Christian sacraments.

> With the approach we have been using, it can become clear that the sacraments precisely as signs are causes of grace, that it is the case here of causation by symbols, of the kind that belongs to what by its very nature is a symbol. By such "natural symbols" or intrinsically real symbols, we mean, for our purposes here, the spatio-temporal, historical phenomenon, the visible and tangible form in which something that appears, notifies its presence, and by so doing makes itself present, bodying forth this manifestation really distinct from itself. With

natural symbols, the sign or symbol as a phenomenon is intrinsically linked to what it is a phenomenon of, and which is present and operative, even though really distinct. In fact we must distinguish between two aspects: the dependence of the actual manifestation on what is manifesting itself and the difference between the two.[18]

Students of Heidegger will undoubtedly note the resemblance of Rahner's thought to the approach taken by Heidegger. We mentioned this Heideggerian approach above, and at times Rahner's very language resembles that of Heidegger. Rahner is calling for a study of symbol and the ways in which a symbol not only bears witness to the reality it symbolizes but also to the symbolic efficiency of making the reality present.

When one says that a symbol causes an effect, one is saying that a symbol does this in its very signing or symbolic dynamism. The signing, the symbolizing, is in itself causative. This is quite foreign to the traditional theologizing on cause in the Roman Catholic Church and therefore this is the reason why Rahner's approach is so innovative. One does not analyze causality in general, based, for instance, on the Aristotelian framework. Rather, one starts from the dynamism of symbol. Let us consider this in some depth.

John Shea, who has written rather widely on religious symbolism, gathers together a number of ideas from R. Haughton, S. Keen, L. Gilkey, and G. Baum and writes: "The religious symbol does not 'sit' awkwardly on human experience, brought in as an afterthought by an act of piety. This symbol is not a needless decoration, but part of the experience explicating its richness and declaring its fullness . . . It can be told to others, and if they live within the symbol and surrender to its vision they can participate in the experience which gave it birth."[19] Notice the words: explicating and declaring, on the one hand, and, on the other, living within, surrendering to, participating in. In symbols, there is more than mere communication (signing); there is dynamic, resultant action (causing).

Our English word *symbol* is borrowed directly from the Greek word *symbolon*. This Greek word *symbolon* had in classical Greek a variety of meanings, such as:

1. Tally, i.e., each of two halves of a piece of pottery
2. Complementary factors
3. A seal-impression on wax
4. Any token serving as a proof of identity
5. Credentials
6. Guarantee
7. Token of good will
8. An identity token given to an Athenian dicaster on entering the court, which entitled him to vote; on presenting this first *symbolon* for voting privilege he would receive a second *symbolon* which could be exchanged for the fee.
9. At Rome, a token entitling the bearer to a donation of money
10. A passport
11. A passenger list
12. A treaty
13. A contract between individuals
14. A receipt made out in duplicate
15. A fee for making out a receipt

There is not one item which undergirds each and every one of these meanings of *symbolon,* but there is an item which undergirds the majority of these usages, namely, the notion of duality: there is one item (A) which has a relationship to another item (B) and the two form some sort of unity. In the first meaning, "Tally," we are dealing with a piece of pottery, more precisely, two halves of a piece of pottery. The transaction was written on the pottery, and when dried was broken in two. One party of the transaction kept half; the other party kept the second half. On completion of the transaction, the bearer of the one half and the bearer of the second half compared the two halves, and if they fit together, the final payments were then made.

Herodotus, in his *History,* offers the following story which indicates this method of using *symbola.* Leotychides tells a story to the Athenians, Herodotus writes, about an incident over a pledge which once took place in Sparta. There was in Sparta a noble gentleman named Glaucus and it happened once that a person from Miletus came to him and made the following offer:

> I am of Miletus, and I have come hither, Glaucus, in the hope of profiting by thy honesty. For when I heard much talk thereof in Ionia and through all the rest of Greece, and when I observed that whereas Ionia is always insecure, but the Pelopennese stands firm and unshaken, and when I noted likewise how wealth is continually changing hands in our country, I took counsel with myself and resolved to turn one-half of my substance into money and place it in thy hands, since I am well assured that it will be safe in thy keeping. Here then is the silver—take it—and take likewise these tallies [*symbola*]; be careful of them; remember thou art to give the money to the person who shall bring you their [the symbols'] fellows.[20]

The story goes on to note that many years later the sons of this man from Miletus returned to Glaucus, presented their portion of the tallies (*symbola*), and requested the money which had been left with Glaucus. Glaucus at first demurred and told them to return in four months, for as he said, "I have no recollection of such a transaction." However, Glaucus consulted the oracle at Delphi, asking whether he should simply deny everything and pretend no knowledge of the former transaction and thereby retain the money. The oracle, however, spoke of justice and the punishment of injustice. Glaucus was touched, sent for the Milesian strangers, and since the two pieces of pottery coincided he returned the money to them. Nevertheless, since he had tempted the gods with the idea of gaining money, his entire family line died out.

This story from Herodotus has a use of symbols which one finds in other works of classical Greek literature, such as *Medea.* The joining together of the two halves of the clay tablet is clearly not the money, but indicates and makes evident that the money belongs to the Milesian strangers. In other words, something happens at one level—the joining of the halves of pottery—and something else far more important happens at a deeper level: the sign and the reality, the *sacramentum* and the *res sacramenti*.

With the Athenian dicaster (no. 8 above), the situation is similar. The one who has the right to vote has sent his part of the *symbolon* ahead; the proxy shows his piece of pottery to the official, and if they correspond, the proxy may cast a vote. On voting, the proxy receives a piece of pottery; when given to the paymaster who has the other half, he receives his fee for being a proxy.

With the passenger list, the case is similar. One purchases the "ticket," in this case receiving one half of a piece of pottery, which, if presented to the shipmaster at the time of sailing, allows passage.

It is this two-level dynamic which is at the heart of a symbol: the sign level and the reality level. In the sacramental action, what one sees, hears, touches, feels, or perceives is only the sign; beneath the perceptible is the reality. There are, however, two kinds of such sign-reality events:

(1) In the first instance, the sign becomes superfluous once the reality has been attained. The two are quite separable. For instance a map is needed to reach a particular destination; once the destination has been attained, the map is superfluous. The map is the sign pointing to the reality of the destination.

(2) In the second instance, a sign or symbol is always needed to reveal the reality. For instance, all the signs of love, e.g., kissing, embracing, etc., reveal the reality of love, but the love itself is never experienced except in and through such signs.

This latter is the case with the sacraments. The reality is never attained directly; the sacramental sign is needed both to announce the presence of a reality (God's grace and presence) and to make it effective in some way or another. Let us consider this in greater detail, with the proviso, however, that what follows is merely meant to be a sort of theological reflection and suggestion.[21] It cannot be construed as the "teaching" of the Church. Still, one must realize that none of the theories on sacramental causality are put forth officially as the "teaching of the Church." How sacraments "effect" grace remains an open theological question, as we saw above.

In contemporary theological works on grace, grace is not seen as a "thing," but as "presence" or a "relationship."[22] In Scholastic theology, grace was considered as a thing: created grace, which was then divided into actual and habitual, *elevans* and *sanans,* merely salutary and efficacious, etc. All of these graces were different kinds of created grace. Because of this emphasis, one could speak of "gaining grace" and "losing grace," of "meriting grace" and "state of grace." If grace is considered a "thing," in some way or another, then the phrase "sacraments effect grace" will have a definite, "thing"-effecting causality. If, on the other hand, grace is considered a "relationship," then we are dealing more with uncreated grace, God, than with created grace, and if God is already related to us, then the sacraments will "cause" an intensification of this relationship. Things can be seen in the context of either-or: either one is in the state of sanctifying grace or not; either one has efficacious grace or not. Relationships, once they are established, are rather more-or-less realities: one grows more in love with one's spouse; children come to love their parents more. In this relational reference, sacraments "cause" a deepening or intensification of an already present relationship.

Let us consider this "thing/relation" aspect of grace from the standpoint of the Scholastic (thing) interpretation of several sacraments, using terminology which is quite traditional, and then look at the same situation from a relational reference.

1. *Baptism.* Baptism is said to take away original sin and give us sanctifying grace. These ideas fit well with an infant baptism, but in the case of an adult baptism these ideas are not operable. In the Scholastic theology of sacraments, an

adult faced only two alternatives to one's life: heaven or hell. For an adult, there was no "limbo," which means that an adult would not be sent to hell simply for original sin, nor could an adult enter heaven if there were original sin. One went to hell for serious, actual sins, and one went to heaven with no sin whatsoever. For an adult, original sin had been taken away, long before baptism and long before even the desire of baptism. This also means that long before baptism or even the desire of baptism, an adult had received sanctifying grace or perhaps lost sanctifying grace (the only reason one goes to hell). What, then, does baptism do in the case of an adult?

2. *Penance.* It is the teaching of St. Thomas Aquinas that the absolution of a priest is given to someone who is already contrite. Poschmann writes:

> Going beyond the doctrine, which was general from the time of Abelard, that the will to submit to the tribunal of ecclesiastical penance is an indispensable element of true contrition, he [Thomas] claims that contrition derives its power of obtaining forgiveness of sin from the absolution subsequently bestowed. The reason is that only through absolution is the fruit of the passion of Christ communicated to the penitent as he co-operates with grace in the destruction of sin—*ad destructionem peccati* (S. th. III q. 84, a 5). He [Thomas] is not thinking here merely of some kind of substitute for the sacrament by a desire of it which is efficacious *ex opere operantis* in the sense of later theology, but of a second mode of true sacramental operation. The sacrament operates not only in act, but also in the intention of receiving it (*proposito*). *Sacramentum in proposito* (*voto*) *existens*, so runs the constantly recurring expression. The theory is not the exclusive property of Aquinas. In its elements it was already proposed by his teacher, Albert (IV Sent. d. 11, a. 1 ad 6; d. 18 a 1 ad 1; a 7 *resp.*). Alexander, on the other hand, and St. Bonaventure reject it. In fact it is untenable.[23]

For St. Thomas, the normal situation is the bestowal of absolution on someone whose sins have already been forgiven. What, then, does the sacrament of penance add to forgiveness already attained?

3. *Eucharist.* Vatican II and Pope Paul VI spoke about the many presences of Jesus: his presence in the gathered community, his presence in the proclamation of the word, his presence in the life of grace. These are all "presences" which most often precede the Eucharistic prayer and therefore the Eucharistic presence of Jesus. If Jesus is already present, prior to the Eucharistic prayer, in what way is he newly present?

These are all situations and questions which deserve an answer, and they need to be taken up in detail with the individual sacraments involved. There are similar situations and questions which involve the other sacraments as well, not simply these three, which are used only for the sake of examples.

In sacraments, we indeed celebrate God's presence, God's forgiving presence, God's forgiving grace. Yet this presence and forgiveness and grace are already in our lives *prior* to the celebration of a sacrament. We also believe that this presence, forgiveness and grace remain with us long after the actual celebration of a sacrament. It would seem then that in a sacramental celebration we are celebrating:

1. what God has been doing;
2. what God is presently doing;
3. what God will continue to do.

In baptism we celebrate the grace of life; in penance we celebrate the grace of reconciliation; in the Eucharist we celebrate the grace of Jesus' presence; in anointing we celebrate the grace of God's healing power; and so on. In this sense the sacraments are signs: they reveal the reality of God's presence, God's forgiveness and God's grace. But sacraments do more than that. This "more" is what we specify when we say that sacraments "cause grace."

In the example we used above of a sign which was always needed to reveal the reality, namely, the signs of love, e.g., the kiss, the embrace, etc., it should be noted not only that (hopefully) the kiss and the embrace reveal the love that one person has for another, but also that the very kissing and the very embracing enhance, deepen and transform the mutual love. The word "transform" is perhaps the better term to use in the case of sacramental celebration. In the celebrating of a sacrament, not only are God's love, presence, forgiveness and grace revealed, but these are enhanced, deepened and transformed. It is precisely this dimension which is involved when one says that sacraments "cause" grace. The signing not only reveals but transforms and deepens; this transforming and deepening is present only in the signing. The sacraments in no way act "magically" or "automatically," just as neither a kiss nor an embrace acts "magically" or "automatically." Rather, they are the media in and through which God's very presence and love is both revealed and deepened, just as the kiss and the embrace are the media through which human love is revealed and deepened. In many ways this position is close to "occasional" causality, described above. Just as the kiss and the embrace are the "occasions" of manifesting and enhancing one's love for another, so, too, *mutatis mutandis,* the sacraments are the occasions for revealing and transforming our relationship with God. In this view, then, both sign and "cause" are brought together, in the way that Rahner suggests, and the sacramental action remains completely God's work, and therefore totally gift or grace, since even the "occasions" are due to God's initiative, not our human initiative.

Perhaps the phrase "sacrament of the cause" might be a better way of describing this sacramental action: the cause remains God; the rituals of word and action are, again by God's design, the signs of his causing, not because of any intrinsic necessity in either the words or the actions, but because of God's own economy. Moreover, in this economy, God has determined that the reality of his presence will be manifest only in and through the sign or sacrament, on these given occasions. In other words, the sign-reality relation-

ship, by God's design, are so bound together that the one is
present only in and through the other.

5. Summary

1. Sacramental causality is basically the relationship between grace and good works, and must be theologically explained in this light.

2. St. Thomas systematized a form of sacramental causality which has been called instrumental, efficient causality.
The instrument depends on the primary agent, but it also has
its own (secondary) efficient effect.

3. At the time of the Reformation, particularly with Melchior Cano, a moral causality of the sacraments was developed. The sacraments are seen as prayers and not as acting
in any efficient way.

4. A third way of considering sacramental activity is
called occasional causality. The sacramental rite is a sign of
God's intentions, which God has foreordained.

5. None of these views were officially accepted by the
Council of Trent. The question of sacramental causality remains a theologically open question.

6. Karl Rahner has attempted to bring together the sacraments as signs and the sacraments as causes. In the past
Catholic theologians kept the sign and cause aspects of the
sacraments apart.

7. Rahner's view is substantiated by the basic meaning
of the Greek word *symbolon* and its usage in classical Greek
literature.

8. Some symbols become unnecessary once the reality
has been attained. Other symbols must always be present,
since the reality to which they point can only be present in
and through a symbol. The analogy of human love is helpful
in understanding this latter situation.

9. In some ways sacraments celebrate (a) what God has been doing, (b) what God is presently doing, (c) what God will continue to do. The causality of the sacraments makes these three aspects of God's activity evident in the sacramental action.

Discussion Questions

1. What is the theological understanding of efficient, instrumental causality of the sacraments?
2. What is the theological understanding of moral causality of the sacraments?
3. What is the theological understanding of occasional causality of the sacraments?
4. How would you explain that "sacraments give grace"?

Chapter Five

Jesus as Primordial Sacrament

THIS CHAPTER DEALS WITH SOMETHING WHICH IS RATHER NEW in Catholic theology, namely, Jesus himself as a sacrament. We have already alluded to this above, but let us now consider the matter in more detail. Semmelroth, Rahner and Schillebeeckx were the theologians who focused Catholic attention on the matter of Jesus as a primordial sacrament. The Second Vatican Council did not make any mention of Jesus as a sacrament, but it is somewhat presumed throughout its consideration of the Church as a sacrament. The understanding of Jesus as a sacrament is central to contemporary Roman Catholic theology and practice of the sacraments.

Let us consider the matter from the following viewpoints:

1. Jesus, in his humanity, as a sacrament.
2. Jesus as the primordial or fundamental sacrament.
3. Jesus as sacrament and Christology.

1. Jesus, in His Humanity, as a Sacrament

It cannot be stressed enough that Jesus can only be considered as a sacrament in and through his human nature. In all sacramental discussion, there is the sacrament, and there is the reality to which the sacrament refers. The reality is always superior to the sacrament. It is for this reason, above all, that the humanity alone can be the focus of Jesus as sacrament. If the divine nature of Jesus is the sacrament, then there is a reality superior to the divine nature, which is an unacceptable position in Christian theology. If the second person of the Trinity is the sacrament, then the first person, the Father, is superior to the Logos, which again is unacceptable to Christian theology. Therefore, it is the human nature of Jesus which is the sacrament of God's presence.

For his part, Rahner describes this sacramentality of Jesus in the following way:

> But now in the Word of God, God's last word is uttered into the visible public history of mankind, a word of grace, reconciliation and eternal life: Jesus Christ. The grace of God no longer comes (when it comes) steeply down from on high, from a God absolutely transcending the world, and in a manner that is without history, purely episodic; it is permanently in the world in tangible, historical form, established in the flesh of Christ as a part of the world, of humanity and of its very history.
>
> This is what we mean by saying that Christ is the actual historical presence in the world of the eschatologically triumphant mercy of God. . . . There is the spatio-temporal sign that effects what it points to. Christ in his historical existence is both reality and sign, *sacramentum* and *res sacramenti,* of the redemptive grace of God, which through him no longer, as it did before his coming, rules high over the world as the as yet hidden will of the remote, transcendent God, but in him is given and established in the world, and manifested there.[1]

Over and over again in this passage Rahner speaks of Jesus in his historical existence, who has come into the visible, public history of humanity, who is present in tangible, historical form. All of this refers to the humanity of Jesus, that is, his historical humanity which he enjoyed in Palestine, and the risen humanity which he has in heaven.

This humanity is the *sacramentum,* that is, the sign, or symbol, or perceptible, tangible, visible reality. Again, this is Jesus' humanity, which is for us perceptible, tangible, visible. In this sacramental presence, Jesus is also the *res sacramenti,* that is, the reality to which the sacrament refers, namely, the presence of divinity itself, the divine grace of reconciliation and eternal life. This *res sacramenti* is not the humanity of Jesus but the divinity, is not the human person of Jesus (if we might speak that way) but the divine person. A sacramental event requires both the sacrament (sign, symbol) and the reality. The two-nature Christology involves this: the human nature as the sacrament and the divine nature as the reality or, in Latin, the *res sacramenti.*

Schillebeeckx is even clearer on this issue than Rahner. As Schillebeeckx begins his section on *Christ the primordial sacrament,* he states very clearly:

> The dogmatic definition of Chalcedon, according to which Christ is "one person in two natures," implies that one and the same person, the Son of God, also took on a visible human form. Even in his humanity Christ is the Son of God. The second person of the most holy Trinity is personally man; and this man is personally God.[2]

This is the foundation for Schillebeeckx, and for all who present Jesus as a sacrament: the incarnation of the divine Logos in the humanity of Jesus. Given this foundation, one can then go on to the sacramentality of Jesus:

> The man Jesus, as the personal visible realization of the divine grace of redemption, is *the* sacrament, the primordial sacrament, because this man, the Son of God himself, is intended by the Father to be in his humanity the only way to the actuality of redemption.[3]

Schillebeeckx's stress on the humanity of Jesus as the locus of sacramentality is paramount and must be stressed, so that a clear understanding of Jesus as sacrament can be appreciated. If Jesus' human nature is a sacrament, then one must ask: *Of what* is Jesus' human nature a sacrament? Rahner and Schillebeeckx give a variety of answers, which we find in the citations above:

Rahner: grace, reconciliation, eternal life
           the grace of God
           the eschatologically triumphant mercy of God
           the redemptive grace of God
Schillebeeckx: the divine grace of redemption
           the only way to the actuality of redemption

Jesus' humanity, as a sacrament, evidently centers around God's loving and redeeming grace for all men and women. The words which one might employ can be varied, but it seems that the reality is clearly God's redemptive love for us: redemptive because it is forgiving, love because it is grace. All that God has intended, is intending and will intend for men and women is sacramentally referred to in the humanity of Jesus.

Jesus, however, is not simply a sign of this redemptive love; he brings it, he makes it present, he therefore *effects* it. Sacraments are both signs and causes, as we have seen, and again, as we noted above, it is in the very signing that the sacrament causes, and it is in causing that the sacrament signs. Jesus is the effective sacrament of our redemption.

How has Jesus, in and through his humanity, done this? First of all one should cite his message: his words, his parables, his preaching. Biblical scholars today try to highlight what Jesus himself preached, while he was alive in Palestine. Since Jesus did not preach about himself, then there is a difference between (a) what Jesus preached and (b) what the New Testament preaches about Jesus. In our Christian Bible we have only the latter, and one must attempt to go beneath the New Testament data and cull out what Jesus' own message might have been. One biblical scholar who has done this rather well is Jeremias, who expresses the message of Jesus, *as he preached it,* in the following way:[4]

1. The return of the quenched Spirit
2. Overcoming the rule of Satan

3. The dawn of the reign of God
4. Good news for the poor

Each of these points which Jeremias makes as the substance of Jesus' own preaching overlaps and fleshes out one another. Most authors claim that the kingdom is the main theme of Jesus' preaching, and Jeremias clearly goes along with this. It was, he notes, the belief of many pious Jews at the time of Jesus, that the Spirit of God which had not raised up a prophet in Israel since the deaths of Haggai, Malachai and Zechariah, would return in the "last days," that is, at the time of the final messianic kingdom. Jesus preached that the Spirit of God had returned in himself; therefore the kingdom he announced was indeed the final kingdom of the messianic age.

The triumph of this messianic age, however, has a flipside: the definitive end of satanic power. Evil is in no way the final answer to human life; rather, the grace of the final kingdom of God is the ultimate answer, a final kingdom in which evil (therefore Satan) will have no power whatsoever. This "overcoming of the rule of Satan" was clearly a part of the message of Jesus as regards the kingdom.

This kingdom is not, however, a narrow kingdom. One of the most striking features of Jesus' message is his proclamation of salvation to the poor, that is, those who were rejected by Jesus' opponents. These outcasts are called publicans, prostitutes, sinners. Such people at the time of Jesus included all those who were engaged in despised trades and whose way of life was disreputable. The kingdom of God, which Jesus preached, included even these marginated peoples.

In brief, then, if we follow Jeremias, this is the sum and substance of what Jesus taught. However, there is more. Jesus' actions also were a sign of this message of redemptive grace: his way of life which was poor and humble, his healings, his persecution which included his arrest and trial, his rejection by both Jewish and Roman leadership, his dying in an ignominious way on the cross. Both Jesus' words and his actions have to be seen as *sacrament.* In other words, his total human, historical existence was a sacrament of God's forgiving grace.

This message, which Jesus both preached and lived, is clearly repeated in the New Testament. The faith of Jesus' followers, after the resurrection, added in a most explicit way that Jesus was Lord, that is, God. It is this *explicit preaching* of Jesus as Lord which differentiates between the preaching of Jesus during his lifetime and the preaching about Jesus by the early Christian communities. All of this is, of course, revelation, since all of this is found in the New Testament as the word of God.

After the resurrection, Jesus is no longer visible, tangible, perceptible. After the resurrection, the Church begins to function as sacrament, which we shall consider in the next chapter. This does not mean that Jesus, in his risen body, is no longer the primordial sacrament, nor that he was only a sacrament while he was alive in Palestine. The relationship is more intricate and complex. Jesus, risen in glory, remains the primordial sacrament, but to understand this we will have to take up the issue of the Church as a basic sacrament, the theme of the next chapter.

One other item, however, remains in this first section on Jesus, in his humanity, as sacrament: namely, *for whom* is Jesus a sacrament? It is at the very center of the Christian faith that Jesus died for all men and women. This is the classical expression of this dogma. This classical formula means several things. First of all, it means that there is no salvation for any man or woman, outside of Jesus Christ. The salvation of the entire world is somehow related to Jesus Christ. When one considers world religions other than Christianity, in which Jesus plays or has played no role whatsoever, the complexity of the statement, "Outside Jesus Christ there is no salvation," becomes immediately evident. This teaching is a fundamental part of Christology, and it would become too involved to treat in this present context.

Second, the phrase means that the life, death and resurrection of Jesus are all involved in this redemptive action of God. Although the classical formula centers on the death—Jesus died for all—solid theology and all of Christian tradition understands this phrase to mean the life, the death, and the resurrection of Jesus. The mystery of the redemption in no way belittles the life or the resurrection of Jesus in order to favor the death of Jesus. How the life, death and resurrection all fit together is again one of the fundamental issues in Christology, and theologians have varied in their reflections on this. Once again, the complexity of the issue is underscored by this interfacing of life, death and resurrection.

In total agreement with both Scripture and tradition is the Christian belief that all men and women are included in this redemptive and grace-filled process. It is on this basis that one can say that Jesus is a sacrament *for* all men and women, none excepted. Jesus is a sacrament, therefore, for Christian and non-Christian, those in the Church and those not connected to the Church. Jesus is a sacrament *of* the kingdom and *for* the kingdom.

2. Jesus as the Primordial or Fundamental Sacrament

Contemporary Catholic theologians assert more than the mere statement that Jesus in his humanity is a sacrament. They also maintain that Jesus, in his humanity, is the primordial or fundamental sacrament. The precise term used by theologians does indeed vary: some prefer primordial, others fundamental, others basic, others root-sacrament, in German *Ursakrament* or *Grundsakrament*. Since this notion is somewhat new, a jockeying of terminology is still going on, but all of these terms center around a similar idea, namely, that Jesus is *the basic sacrament* in the Christian Church. The implications of this kind of thinking have not yet permeated Catholic sacramental thought. Vaillancourt refers to such implications when he writes: "The first impact of the Christological renewal on sacramental theology is to make us see the sacraments in the perspective of the sacramental nature of Christ himself."[5]

Jesus as primordial sacrament means that all other Christian sacraments have their meaning *only* in and through Jesus' sacramentality. This means that the Church is fundamentally and only a sacrament because Jesus is a sacrament. Baptism is fundamentally and only a sacrament because Jesus is a sacrament. Confirmation is a sacrament fundamentally and only because Jesus is a sacrament, and so on. A strict seven-sacrament theology is no longer in place. Rather than a system in which seven rituals are involved, with their own definition and function, sacraments can only be understood in a fundamentally Jesus-as-sacrament system. No longer does a definition of sacrament which applies only to seven rituals provide a unity to the sacraments; it is presently the very sacramentality of Jesus' humanity which unifies the Christian sacraments.

We might exemplify this in the following way. Prior to Vatican II and its theological milieu, one might hear the word "baptism" and think immediately of water. One might hear the word "confirmation" and think of oil. One might hear the word "Eucharist" and think immediately of bread and wine, and so on. In the Scholastic theology of sacrament, the matter and the form often defined the sacrament. In this contemporary approach, when one hears the word "baptism" one should think of Jesus; when one hears the word "confirmation" one should think of Jesus; when one hears the word "Eucharist" one should think of Jesus, and so on. If Jesus is the primordial, fundamental, basic, root sacrament, then it is only *because* he is sacrament that these others can be sacraments. The most basic component of baptism as a sacrament is Jesus; the most basic component of confirmation as a sacrament is Jesus; and so on.

In all of this Jesus becomes, therefore:

THE BAPTIZED ONE	=	JESUS
THE CONFIRMED ONE	=	JESUS
THE REALLY PRESENT ONE	=	JESUS
THE RECONCILER	=	JESUS
THE PRIEST	=	JESUS
THE LOVER	=	JESUS
THE HEALER	=	JESUS

In other words, primordiality is a two-way street: (a) Jesus as sacrament grounds and gives basis to such sacraments as baptism, confirmation, etc., but (b) baptism, confirmation, etc., find their fullest expression in Jesus. The definition of baptism is not to be found in baptism but in Jesus; the definition of confirmation is not to be found in confirmation but in Jesus; the definition of the real presence in the Eucharist is not to be found in the Eucharist but in Jesus, and so on. This is clearly a radically different approach to sacraments than that taken by Scholastic theology, nor has this way of thinking permeated completely into the Christian communities. Bishops, priests and teachers at times still fall back on Scholastic theology and its thought patterns. Jesus as primordial sacrament does not simply mean that alongside of the other sacraments we also have Jesus as a sacrament. Nor does it mean that we are using the term in an analogous way. Jesus, in contemporary theology, is not presented as the "analogical" sacrament but as the primordial sacrament, the root-sacrament. A root is not analogous to a vine, but the very source out of which the vine both defines itself and lives. So, too, with Jesus. Other Christian sacraments define themselves by the sacramentality of Jesus and live from that very sacramentality.

As yet this way of thinking has not been elaborately developed by Catholic theologians. In subsequent volumes dealing with the individual sacraments I will attempt to explore this way of thinking as far as each sacrament is concerned. For our present purposes, it is sufficient to be aware of the implications which this term "primordial" expresses when applied to Jesus as a sacrament vis-à-vis the other Christian sacraments.

3. Jesus as Sacrament and Christology

It may be quite evident by now that a solid understanding of sacramental theology presupposes a solid understanding of Christology. This new approach to Jesus as sacrament, however, indicates certain aspects of Christology which need to be highlighted or emphasized in this Christological background. The main such aspects, in my view, would be the following:

1. *The Humanity of Jesus.* Today there is a growing emphasis on the humanity of Jesus within various Christologies. Indeed, this stress on the humanity of Jesus has been seen, by some, as a concern or even a danger. To stress the humanity of Jesus rather than his divinity might even be judged a diminution of Jesus' full divinity. The sacramentality of Jesus' humanity clearly brings balance to this human emphasis, since the more that the very humanity of Jesus is seen as the sacrament of the divine, the more clearly one joins humanity and divinity. If we would use the traditional sacramental concepts, we can distinguish the *sacramentum tantum* (the sacrament alone), the *res* (the reality) and the *res sacramenti* (the combination of the two). Actually, the very concept of *sacramentum tantum* is unintelligible, since to be a sacrament something or someone must be a sacrament *of* something and *for* someone. Otherwise, it is simply another entity among others. It is precisely this relationality to the *of* and to the *for* that is at the heart of sacramentality, so that there is always a relationship to the *res*.

Similarly, the *res* alone has no sacramental meaning, since in the case of the Christian sacraments, the reality would remain unknown unless a revelation were made to us in word and sacrament (both signs) which adapted themselves to our intelligence. If God did not speak our language in revelation, we would never be a hearer of his word. The reality of God's grace, forgiveness and presence comes to us in and through signs which we call word and sacrament.

This leaves, of course, the combination: *res et sacramentum*. When the humanity of Jesus is seen as only a sacrament (*sacramentum tantum*), it would have little meaning. Jesus is, in such a case, only another human being among many. Without revelation on the other hand through word and sacrament, we would never understand God, even in a limited way. Thus an exclusive focus on the divinity of Jesus can become abstract and to all purposes meaningless. Jesus as sacrament, however, is quite a different focus, for in and through the humanity of Jesus we begin to see a God who is credible, namely, the same God to whom Jesus prayed, whom he preached, and whom he obeyed. Indeed, the very God which became incarnate in him.

The humanity of Jesus, as the sacrament of God's love, preserves the best and the most solid in both the humanness and the divinity of the incarnate Lord.

2. *Jesus as Savior.* It is remarkable that the central mystery of Christianity, Jesus as Savior of the world, has never been the immediate focus of any solemn and official teaching of the Church. The creeds express this mystery in a very brief way, using biblical terminology. The earliest creeds simply recount that Jesus was crucified, died, buried, rose and ascended (cf. Hippolytus, Psalter of Aethelstanus, Codex Laudianus, etc.[6]). The earliest Eastern creeds elaborate slightly on these kinds of declarative statements by saying that "for us men and women and for our salvation," Jesus became flesh and was crucified, etc. In all of these, the phrasing is terse and close to New Testament language. On the other hand, the one person–two nature understanding of Jesus received enormous theological consideration and eventually conciliar declarations. The contrast between official and sol-

emn statements on the incarnation and the lack of such statements on the redemption has been noted again and again by theologians.[7]

Over the centuries, theologians have developed theories to help one understand the meaning of the redemption. These theories emphasize one aspect over another in this redemptive process, but generally not in any exclusive way. Contemporary authors such as J. Rivière have provided us with histories of this doctrine of redemption and have attempted to categorize these various theological theories.[8] The lists are not always the same, of course, but in the main they tend to cluster around three emphases:

1. Jesus, in his redemptive work, is seen as a *victor;*
2. Jesus, in his redemptive work, is seen as a *victim;*
3. Jesus, in his redemptive work, is seen as a *revealer.*

A great many of the early Fathers of the Church stressed Jesus as victor. In his book *Christus Victor,* Gustaf Aulén writes: "The central idea of *Christus Victor* is the view of God and the Kingdom of God as fighting against evil powers ravaging mankind. In this drama Christ has the key role, and the title *Christus Victor* says the decisive word about his role."[9] This approach is called by Aulén the classical approach and enjoys the backing of Origen, Athanasius, Basil, Gregory of Nyssa, Gregory Nazianzen, Cyril of Alexandria, Cyril of Jerusalem, and John Chrysostom. These are all Eastern theologians, but the Western theologians such as Ambrose, Augustine, Leo the Great, Gregory the Great and others are mentioned also by Aulén as proponents of this *victor* view of redemption.

The *victim* theory has its roots in Tertullian and Cyprian, with their approach to penance and the transference of merit. It is, of course, Anselm who systematizes this theory in his well-known book: *Cur Deus Homo.* Anselm influenced the Middle Ages and Latin theology generally in an overpowering way. The victim theory or the atonement theory in which Jesus offers vicarious satisfaction to God for sinful men and women became almost commonplace in the West. Thomas Aquinas clarified even further the approach Anselm had systematized. "The payment of satisfaction is treated as the essential element in Atonement and as accomplished by the death of Christ; the payment is primarily the work of Christ's human nature, but it gains increased meritorious value on account of the union of human nature with the Divine nature in Christ. So Thomas Aquinas teaches explicitly: the human nature of Christ makes the offering, but, because He is God, the merit of His work is not merely sufficient, but superabundant."[10] In fact, because of the divine nature it is more than superabundant, it is infinite. This *victim* theory became fairly standard in Catholic thought, and even the *Baltimore Catechism* repeated it: "By the Redemption is meant that Jesus Christ, as the Redeemer of the whole human race, offered His sufferings and death to God as a fitting sacrifice in satisfaction for the sins of men, and regained for them the right to be children of God and heirs of heaven."[11]

The *revealer* theory is strong in the Johannine writings and in Clement of Alexandria as well as Origen. Thus it has, as all the other redemptive theories do, both New Testament and patristic roots. However, it is generally associated with Peter Abelard and his critique of the Anselmian approach. Abelard, however, did not get much of a hearing in the Middle Ages for a variety of theological and political reasons. There seems to be more interest in him since the writings of Schleiermacher, Ritschl and Rashdall, on the one hand, and on the other hand since the renewed biblical studies on the meaning of grace in St. Paul and in the Johannine writings. Revelation as grace and salvation as grace enjoy, today, a certain emphasis.

These three foci of redemption continue to attract attention in our own day. Officially the Church has not endorsed any of them, but one can readily see that an underlying theme in this whole matter of redemption or salvation is the interfacing of grace and human work. As far as Jesus is concerned, we are dealing with the interfacing of grace and Jesus' human work: his very life, death and resurrection. *Grace and good works* was one of the major issues of the Reformation and a major topic of the Council of Trent as we see in the *Decree on Justification*. It is precisely this issue of grace and good works which galvanized the Reformation and Counter-Reformation theology of sacraments. The reformers criticized the Roman Church for its magical and manipulative sacramental theology; the Roman Church countered with its sacramental theology, expressed in the Council of Trent.

Without any intention of being simplistic, I would suggest that there are some connections between the following topics:

1. the *Victim* theory of redemption and instrumental, efficient causality in sacramental theology;

2. the *Victor* theory and moral causality in sacramental theology;

3. the *Revealer* theory of redemption and the occasional causality theory of sacramental causality.

Such connections as expressed so forthrightly above are indeed simplistic and would need a great deal of clarification. On the other hand, there seems to be some interconnection between the way in which one understands the redemptive action of Jesus and the "redemptive action" of sacraments. For instance, in the *Victim* theory Jesus in many ways is presented as acting, in his human nature, instrumentally and efficiently. In the *Victor* theory, Jesus, again in his human nature, is seen as presenting a moral victory over evil, with God, of course, being the decisive and final victor over evil. In the *Revealer* theory Jesus is the occasion in which God reveals to us his saving love. All of this needs to be worked out more in detail, a task more suited to Christology than a theology on the sacraments.

It would seem that the presentation of Jesus as sacrament

can aid both the Christian understanding of redemption and the way in which God and Christ act in the sacraments. The life, death and resurrection, from their human aspects, are the "sacrament" of God's saving work. Jesus was "sacrament" in and through his life, death and resurrection. So, too, the Christian sacraments are the signs of this continuing salvific work within the ecclesial community. In this sacramental approach both as far as the redemption of humankind in Jesus is concerned and as far as the ecclesial sacramental activity is concerned, God's grace, that is, his free gift, remains paramount, and the "good work" is seen as revelatory and as deepening or transforming our response to this initial work of God. I would suggest that this fairly new approach to Jesus as sacrament might be of valuable help in rethinking the meaning of redemption and bring, thereby, the redemptive action of God and Jesus into a closer relationship to sacramental activity in the Church. Since the issue of grace and good works was so central to the Reformation and to the Council of Trent, this "sacramental" approach to Jesus might easily be one of the keys to the current ecumenical dialogue among the various Christian divisions. As long as we stay on only the sacramental level, that is, discussing baptism, Eucharist, ministry, etc., we may not reach new breakthroughs, but if we would refocus our attention on the sacramentality of Jesus, indeed on the primordial sacramentality of Jesus, we might more easily come to far-reaching ecumenical agreements.

It would seem that this contemporary emphasis on Jesus as primordial sacrament would enrich Christology on these two fronts: on a solid appreciation of the humanity of Jesus and on a solid appreciation on the meaning of redemption. This integration has not yet been developed in any strong way, due perhaps to the very newness of the idea of Jesus as primordial sacrament. Still, the more this integration takes place, the richer it will be for Christology and for sacramental theology generally.

4. Summary

We can summarize the main points of this chapter in the following way:

1. Jesus must be considered as the primordial sacrament only in virtue of his human nature. His divinity should not be seen as sacramental in order to avoid any subordinationism.

2. In his humanity, Jesus is the sacrament of all that God wants to give to men and women: his grace, his forgiveness, his love, his presence. This is the *of what* aspect of Jesus' sacramentality.

3. In his humanity, Jesus is a sacrament for all men and women. This is the *for whom* aspect of Jesus' sacramentality. It raises the difficult issue: outside of Jesus Christ there is no salvation for anyone.

4. Jesus is sacrament by what he preached; but he is more than a messenger. His life, death and resurrection are also part of his sacramental activity.

5. Jesus is not simply a sacrament, but he is the primordial sacrament. As such he is the basis why any other Christian aspect can be seen as a sacrament. This intrinsic connection has not yet been fully developed in sacramental theology.

6. Jesus is not a sacrament in an analogous way. A theory of analogy does not do justice to what "Jesus as primordial sacrament" means.

7. Jesus as sacrament helps us understand the full humanity of Jesus without, thereby, belittling his full divinity.

8. Jesus as sacrament helps us understand the meaning of redemption and puts the three main ways of seeing redemption, *victor, victim,* and *revealer,* in a new perspective.

9. Jesus as sacrament underscores the main issue which confronted the Protestant and Catholic dispute at the time of the Reformation: grace and good works. Further study of Je-

sus as sacrament will help resolve some of the difficulties behind this dispute.

Discussion Questions

1. What is meant by Jesus as primordial sacrament?
2. What does the Christian teaching, "outside of Jesus
   Christ there is no salvation," mean?
3. What does "redemption" mean?
4. What does "subordinationism" mean?
5. How would you explain the controversy over grace and
   good works?

Chapter Six

The Church as a Basic Sacrament

PART OF THE ORDINARY MAGISTERIAL TEACHING OF THE Catholic Church today is that the Church itself is a sacrament. The Second Vatican Council, as we saw above, stated this on several occasions. Such statements do not make this approach to the Church part of the infallible teaching of the Church, but they do make this teaching part of the ordinary teaching of the Church for our time.

In order to appreciate this understanding of Church as a sacrament, we will consider three particular items:

1. The Church as a sacrament
2. The Church as a basic sacrament
3. The sacramentality of the Church and ecclesiology

1. The Church as a Sacrament

The Church is fundamentally something we believe in; as the creeds say: "We believe in one, holy, catholic and apostolic Church." If the Church were not something which evoked our faith, we would be left with another institution like a business corporation or a governmental structure. One does not believe in a business corporation such as Exxon, nor does one believe in a country's government, but one must have faith to understand the Church in even an inchoative way. This is why the Church has been seen as a mystery.

The first draft which the bishops studied on the Church during Vatican II, had a section entitled: The Nature of the Church Militant. On October 1, 1963, a new draft was accepted, and this section was now titled: The Mystery of the Church. Some of the bishops—but only a few—were uneasy with this term "mystery." For them a mystery seemed to mean something unknowable; it stressed the invisible Church, not the visible Church. Ever since the Reformation, particularly under the leadership of Bellarmine, the Church in Catholic circles was presented in its visible structures in a very strong way, in contrast to the "Protestant" approach of a hidden Church. Kloppenburg cites an official explanation given to the council bishops at that time: "The word 'mystery,' in this context, does not indicate simply that a thing is unknowable or hidden. Rather, as many authorities recognize today, it points to a transcendent divine reality that has to do with salvation and that is in some sensible way revealed and manifested."[1]

The final and approved form of the constitution on the Church retained this title: "The Mystery of the Church," and the Church as a mystery is repeated in nos. 5, 39, 44, and 63 of this same document. It is also found in other Vatican II decrees: the decree on ecumenism (nos. 2 and 20), the decree on the training of priests (nos. 9 and 16), the decree on the missions (n. 16), the constitution on the Church in the modern world (nos. 2 and 40), and the declaration on the Church's relationship to non-Christian religions (n. 4). Without using the word "mystery" this presentation of the Church is also found in the constitution on the liturgy (nos. 2, 5 and 7). It is abundantly clear that the official Church teaching centers a theology of the Church on "mystery."

However, in order to grasp what the council document wishes to convey, one must begin with the very title of the constitution: *Lumen Gentium* (Light of the World). This light is not the Church; this light is Jesus. The opening sentence of the constitution makes this abundantly clear: "Christ is the light of humanity." The bishops want only to make this light of Christ shine out visibly to all (n. 1). Since men and women are not simply individuals in a privatized sense, but individuals in a community in a social sense, the Church brings this light of Christ to a social or communal world. Even more, the Church itself is a social and communal entity which the Lord himself established through the Holy Spirit. In other words, the message of God in Christ is not a privatized word, but a social and communal word, and the community called Church is not a group of private individuals but a social and communal group. If this social or communitarian aspect of both Jesus as light of the world and the Church as messenger of that light is not understood, neither Jesus nor the Church will be understood. This is the thrust of the Vatican II constitution on the Church.

The Church as a mystery can only be understood if one sees Jesus as the light of the world. If one tries to see the Church itself as the light of the world, one has started off incorrectly. Kloppenburg, in his analysis of the Vatican II document, makes this approach quite clear, when he states that the Church as a mystery is a "mystery of the moon." This metaphor brings out strongly what the council wanted to say.

> We can understand the Church only if we relate it to Christ, the glorified Lord. *The Church lives by Christ.* If the Church is absolutized, separated from Christ, considered only in its structures, viewed only in its history and studied only under its visible, human and phenomenological aspects, it ceases to be a "mystery" and becomes simply one of countless other religious societies or organizations. It does not then deserve our special attention and total dedication.[2]

Kloppenburg then goes on to say that since Christ alone is the light of the world, he is like the sun, which in our galaxy is the source of light. Alongside the sun is the moon, which has no light of its own, but simply reflects the light of the sun.

The moon in its phases reflects in a waxing and waning way the light of Jesus. Didymus the Blind spoke of a "lunar constitution of the Church," and St. Bonaventure spoke of the "dark radiance" of the Church. Only in the measure that the Church reflects Jesus can the Church in any way be a light to the world. In this view the Church becomes wholly Christocentric, or, as Kloppenburg notes, "relativized" alongside Jesus.[3]

This is the picture, "the mystery of the moon," which one must have, if one is to understand the Church as sacrament. The Church is a sign, a symbol, not the reality. The reality is Jesus; the Church is a sign of that reality: sun and moon to express it poetically. *Of what* is the Church a sacrament? The answer is clear: *of Jesus.* Only when the Church reflects Jesus is the Church really Church. This has validity, not only at the top, with the Pope and the bishops, but also at the diocesan level and the parish level. It also has validity at the individual, Christian level. When I, as an individual Christian, say: "I belong to the Church; I am part of the Church," this challenges me to say in a clearer way: "I am part of the Church" *only when* I reflect Jesus. When the parish or diocese says: "We are acting or speaking now as Church," the parish or diocese does so validly *only when* the parish or diocese reflects Jesus, the light of the world. When the bishops or the Pope says: "We are acting or speaking now as Church," they do so validly *only when* they reflect Jesus, the light of the world. The Church in all its aspects stands relativized because of Jesus. In all of this one sees that the individual Christian, the diocese, the parish, the bishops, and the Pope are sacraments of Jesus whenever they reflect the Lord. This *of Jesus* is the key to the sacramentality of the Church.

When one asks the second question: *For whom* is the Church a sacrament? the answer again is: For everyone. When the Church in all its various components reflects Jesus, it does so not only for Christians, but also for all men and women. No longer is Jesus physically present on earth, as he was during his lifetime. We do not see or perceive his risen human form. We now see this risen Lord only in the sacramentality of Jesus, and since the risen Lord is Lord of all, so, too, the Church reflects to all the power and the promise of the resurrection. This *for whom* aspect of the Church's sacramentality is but another way of expressing the mission of the Church. As the *Pastoral Constitution on the Church in the Modern World* expresses it: "The Church is not motivated by an earthly ambition but is interested in one thing only—to carry on the work of Christ under the guidance of the Holy Spirit, for he came into the world to bear witness to the truth, to save and not to judge, to serve and not to be served" (n. 3). This mission of the Church has been called evangelization, bringing the good news of Jesus to all. Christians evangelize each other, Christian to Christian. This can be called the *ad intra* evangelization; but Christians also evangelize those outside the Christian community, and this can be called the *ad extra* evangelization. Together, the evangelizing mission is seen as a mission for all. The Church neither proclaims itself, but rather Jesus and the kingdom, nor does the Church merely focus on its internal membership, but embraces both those inside and outside its ranks in its complete mission.

In all of this, of course, the principle of sacramentality is at work. Sacraments both manifest and camouflage, and the Church as sacrament can both manifest the Lord and be Church or camouflage the Lord and be un-Church. The Church stands beneath the word of God in all things that it does, and is both judged positively and blamed negatively by this criterion: Jesus, the Word of God made manifest in our world.

2. The Church as a Basic Sacrament

Once again, it must be noted that the terminology for this notion of the Church as a basic sacrament is somewhat unsettled. The adjective "basic" is simply one of the adjectives used by theologians. Other words are "ground-sacrament" or "fundamental sacrament." Naturally, Jesus remains *the* basic sacrament, *the* fundamental sacrament. What other word might then be attributed to the Church to indicate its secondary role vis-à-vis Jesus, but its foundational role vis-à-vis other Christian sacraments? Such wording remains in flux. Rahner, for his part, describes this fundamental aspect of the Church's sacramentality as follows:

> The Church is the abiding presence of that primal sacramental word of definitive grace, which Christ is in the world, effecting what is uttered by uttering it in sign. By the very fact of being in that way the enduring presence of Christ in the world, the Church is truly the fundamental sacrament, the well-spring of the sacraments in the strict sense. From Christ the Church has an intrinsically sacramental structure.[4]

Rahner's choice of words needs to be reflected on. Jesus is described as the "primal sacrament." The connection then with Jesus is clearly stated. This connection is called "intrinsic," and therefore not something simply superadded to the very essence of the Church. On the other hand, the sacramental nature of the Church, stemming from this intrinsic connection with Jesus, is in a strict sense the "well-spring" of all other sacramentality in the Church. Once more, we see that an "analogous" relationship between the Church as a sacrament and the other sacraments is not adequate. It is this "well-spring" in a strict sense approach to the Church which describes the Church as a "basic sacrament."

Schillebeeckx says the same thing, but with a different nuance:

> The earthly Church is the visible realization of this saving reality in history [namely, Jesus]. The Church is a visible communion in grace. This communion itself, consisting of members and a hierarchical leadership, is the earthly sign of the triumphant redeeming grace of Christ. The fact must be emphasized that not only the hierarchical Church but also the community of the faithful belong to this grace-giving sign that is the Church. As much in its hierarchy as in the laity the community of the Church is the realization in historical form of the

victory achieved by Christ. The inward communion in grace
with God in Christ becomes visible in and is realized through
the outward social sign. Thus the essence of the Church con-
sists in this, that the final goal of grace achieved by Christ becomes visibly present in the *whole* Church as a visible society.[5]

Schillebeeckx notes that the Church as basic sacrament is
so first of all in a social way, not in an individual way. The
sacramentality of the Church is to be found in the total
Church, the community. One individual does not constitute
the sacramentality of the Church. Further, Schillebeeckx
notes that the sacramentality of the Church cannot be found
simply in its hierarchical structures, which are the episcopal
and papal structures. Nor can they be found in simply the
"lay" structures, i.e., in all those structures which are not
episcopal or papal.[6] The "basicness" of the Church's sacramentality penetrates the total community, and cannot be iso-
lated into an individualized constituent nor into a sectional
constituency.

These ideas of Rahner and Schillebeeckx help us identify
what and where the basic sacramental structure of the
Church might be. They also raise questions which affect ecclesiology quite generally.

One of these issues we have noted again and again:
namely, the inadequacy of an analogous concept of sacramentality when applied to Jesus and the Church over
against the other Christian sacraments. Semmelroth in his
article, "Die Kirche als Sakrament des Heils," addresses this
problematic in the following way.

> Of course, if the Church today takes up this term, "sacrament,"
> in order to describe itself, it means this in an analogous sense;
> not all the elements in the concept of sacrament, which was
> developed for the seven individual sacraments, and which
> were unified since the eleventh century, are realized in the sac-
> rament Church in simply the same way. However, the consti-
> tutive elements of the sacrament are indeed realized in the
> Church [aber die konstitutiven Elemente des Sakramentes
> sind doch in ihr verwirklicht].[7]

It is difficult to see exactly what Semmelroth wishes to say, for on the one hand he speaks about "all the constitutive elements" of a sacrament being realized in the Church as a sacrament, but yet on the other hand he speaks simply about an "analogous" understanding of the Church as a sacrament. One does not generally speak about similar constitutive elements being the same in two realities, e.g., an X and a Y, and then state that they are only analogous. If constitutive elements are found in both X and Y, one should deduce that they are univocal and not analogous.

Perhaps Semmelroth wishes to say that the constitutive elements of sacrament are *applied* analogously to the Church on the one hand and to the individual sacraments on the other. In this case the analogy is simply in the *application*. Nowhere does he say this and it is not at all implied in his essay.

In the same series, *Mysterium Salutis,* but in a later volume, R. Schulte, referring directly back to Semmelroth's essay, repeats the same thing.[8] Schulte, however, does raise some issues that need to be considered: (a) there is the question of the criterion by which one can say that certain Church actions are "sacraments" and others are not; (b) sacraments generally have a certain material element (water, bread, wine, etc.), and therefore one can ask what the "material" element of the Church as sacrament might be; (c) there is the question of the Church acting as Church only in and through sacraments, or are there not other ways in which the Church as sacrament might realize itself? These are all extremely solid points which must be considered in any ecclesiology today that wishes to stress the Church as a basic sacrament.[9]

Both Semmelroth and Schulte seem to accept the definition of sacrament, worked out for the seven sacraments, as normative or at least as unchangeable. It seems to me, however, that with this fairly new approach to sacraments, namely, Jesus as primordial sacrament and the Church as basic sacrament, the very understanding of sacrament in the Christian community needs to be revised. This is not to say that the understanding of sacrament worked out and unified in the eleventh century, as Semmelroth notes, is wrong. In its day and for the purposes of the seven rituals it was quite adequate, but today it is too restricted and narrow. The very words, "primordial" and "basic," imply that the definition of sacrament must be worked out from Jesus and Church and not from the seven rituals. The constitutive elements and the criteria are to be described on the basis of Jesus and Church *qua sacrament,* not from the sacramental rituals. Otherwise, "primordial" and "basic" are emasculated. Not to grasp the quite "revolutionary" factors involved in Jesus as foundational sacrament and Church as basic sacrament is clearly to miss the theological import of this new approach. "Business as usual" can hardly be the motto.

3. The Sacramentality of the Church and Ecclesiology

Obviously, we have already touched on the issue of ecclesiology and this new approach of the Church as a basic sacrament. For all sacraments, Jesus included, we do need an "external sign," something "material," or, better "something perceptible." The incarnation of the Logos constituted the visible, perceptible, bodily humanness of Jesus as the primordial sign. To call this "material" does not seem adequate, since the very term "material" conveys the matter-form approach to sacramentality, whereas Jesus as sacrament conveys an incarnational approach.

Vatican II stressed this incarnational approach to the Church:

> The one mediator, Christ, established and ever sustains here on earth his holy Church, the community of faith, hope and charity, as a visible organization through which he communicates truth and grace to all men. But the society structured with hierarchical organs and the mystical body of Christ, the visible society and the spiritual community, the earthly

Church and the Church endowed with heavenly riches, are not to be thought of as two realities. On the contrary, they form one complex reality which comes together from a human and divine element. For this reason the Church is compared, not without significance, to the mystery of the incarnate Word. As the assumed nature, inseparably united to him, serves the divine Word as a living organ of salvation, so, in a somewhat similar way, does the social structure of the Church serve the Spirit of Christ who vivifies it, in the building up of the body (Eph 4:15).[10]

Commenting on this precise section, A. Grillmeier states that the council in no way adopted J.A. Möhler's notion of perpetual incarnation. There is no extension of the hypostatic union to include the Church as the body of Christ. Leo XIII's *Satis cognitum* and Pius XII's *Mystici Corporis* are both cited by Grillmeier to make clear what Vatican II says. He notes, however, that in Vatican II the analogy to the incarnation is "definitely exploited," so that "the sacramental structure of the Church comes to the fore again and ultimately its incarnational quality also, though now in a clearer way."[11] Vatican II highlights, then, that the sacramentality of Jesus is based on the incarnation and so too the sacramentality of the Church is based, *mutatis mutandis,* on the incarnation. The incarnation is the root for an understanding of constitutive elements of sacramentality, not a theological position worked out by the eleventh century. On his own, Grillmeier notes that this is quite consonant with the whole history of Christology, particularly the Christology which is found in the patristic period.[12]

The Church as sacrament raises the issue of the relationship between the Church and the kingdom. Theologians do not speak about the kingdom as a basic sacrament, and there are no official Church teachings in this direction either. Again, the ecclesiology of Vatican II makes a distinction (not a separation) between Church and kingdom. Indeed, the kingdom of God is of more importance than the Church, so that the Church is once again placed in a relativized position.

The notion of the Church as a sacrament helps bring out the dignity of the Church on the one hand and the mystery of the kingdom on the other. Basically, the kingdom of God is the presence of God in Jesus to all men and women, indeed to the world at large. In some ways, then, the Church must be seen as the sacrament of the kingdom, not in any sense as though there might be an alternate "larger Church," but in the sense that the kingdom is indeed the presence of Christ, the primordial sacrament.

Cardinal Bernardin at the 1983 synod on reconciliation opened his remarks as follows:

> As Christ is the sacrament of God—the visible and incarnate, efficacious and gratuitous bestowal of divine grace and life, so the Church is the sacrament of Christ in human history. Cardinal de Lubac expressed this with clarity many years ago: "If Christ is the sacrament of God, the Church is for us the sacrament of Christ; she represents him, in the full and ancient meaning of the term; she really makes him present." The Church Christ is the visible presence of the invisible Christ; she is regarded as sacramental in the same sense of that term employed by the Council of Trent, which described sacrament as "the visible form of an invisible grace" (DS 1639).[13]

Bernardin does not mention kingdom, it is true, but the presence of grace, the presence of the invisible Christ, is indeed at the heart of the kingdom. The bishops at Vatican II worked strenuously on the interrelationship of many elements:

1. The relationship between the visible and the invisible aspects of the Church, a topic which the sacramentality of the Church helps clarify.

2. The relationship between the Catholic Church and other Christian Churches. Ecclesiality outside the Roman Catholic Church was unequivocally stated. On this point Grillmeier notes: "That the Churches and communities outside the Catholic Church are truly 'Churches' is also to be explained by the notion of sacrament."[14]

3. The relationship between the Church and the kingdom. Kloppenburg notes: "The Church is not the kingdom of God and is not identifiable with the kingdom of God, but is rather its germ and beginning."[15] He then cites numerous passages from the documents of Vatican II to substantiate his assertion. Again, the sacramentality of the Church helps to underscore and clarify this distinction.

Ecclesiology has indeed been enriched by this emphasis on the Church as sacrament. Relationships to Jesus, to its own inner and sacred dimension, to its various divisions, to the kingdom and to the world generally are all areas of this enrichment. The dignity of every baptized Christian is enhanced, since by their very baptism they are, collectively and individually, sacraments of that one who truly is baptized: Jesus. The dignity of Pope, bishop, priest and deacon is deeply enhanced, since each of these, individually and as a college, are basically sacraments of that one hierarch: Jesus. Only when baptized Christians and those among them who are ordained Christians manifest sacramentally the reality of Jesus are they truly living out both baptism and ordination. The Church as a basic sacrament, in many ways, sacramentalizes each and every aspect of Church life, since Church itself can only exist when it sacramentalizes the primordial sacrament, Jesus. This is today an ecclesiology which only exists in schematic form, but as this notion of the Church as sacrament deepens, it can only enhance the very meaning of Church and make Church thereby a far more credible reality than it is even now.

4. Summary

1. To understand the Church as a sacrament, Vatican II instructs us to begin with the understanding of the Church as mystery. The metaphor of the sun and the moon helps us to see what Vatican II is talking about.

2. The Church as the "mystery of the moon" focuses clearly on Jesus as the light of the world. The Church is only Church when it reflects (sacramentalizes) Jesus. Jesus is the key to the sacramentality of the Church.

3. Jesus and all that he means as sacrament is the *of what* is the Church a sacrament. The Church is a sacrament of a sacrament.

4. The Church is a sacrament for all, Christians and non-Christians. This is the *for whom* aspect of the sacramentality of the Church. There is an *ad intra* and an *ad extra* aspect to this *for whom* aspect of the Church.

5. The Church is a basic sacrament, but not in the same way that Jesus is a basic or fundamental sacrament. The precise terminology for this distinction has not yet been found.

6. The Church as a basic sacrament cannot be seen or described when one uses analogy. The Church is a basic sacrament, not an analogous sacrament.

7. Sacrament itself must be defined or described on the basis of Jesus as primordial sacrament and the Church as basic sacrament, not on the basis of the definition worked out by theologians in the eleventh century.

8. Viewing the Church as a basic sacrament is still being integrated into ecclesiology and there are difficulties which must be further overcome and positions which must be clarified. Catholic theology is beginning to do just this, following the lead given by Vatican II.

9. Vatican II urges us to see the sacramentality of the Church in the light of the incarnation, but not in the sense of a perpetual incarnation.

10. The kingdom is not the same as the Church, and the sacramentality of the Church helps us to see the difference, not the separation.

11. The sacramentality of the Church is also very helpful to the ecumenical movement, in which one speaks about "the Church" and the "churches."

1. What is meant by the phrase "the Church is a sacrament"?
2. What is meant by the phrase "the Church is a basic sacrament"?
3. What is analogy? Why is it inadequate when one speaks of Jesus and the Church as sacraments and then goes on to speak of the other sacraments?
4. What is the distinction between the kingdom of God and the Church?

Chapter Seven

Official Church Teaching on the Sacraments

THE FOCUS OF THIS CHAPTER IS TO CONSIDER THE SOLEMN and official teaching of the Roman Catholic Church on the issue of sacramentality in general. We will not consider such official teaching which deals with the individual sacraments. This will be done elsewhere.

First of all, there are a number of books which gather together these official and solemn teachings, but they also include other material as well. Undoubtedly, the primary source has been *Enchiridion Symbolorum, Definitionum et Declarationum de Rebus Fidei et Morum* (*Handbook of Creeds, Definitions and Declarations on Matters of Faith and Morals*).[1] Often this is simply called "Denzinger." This is a compilation of various Church statements in the original languages (Greek and Latin for the most part), first edited by H. Denzinger in 1854, with its latest edition under the editorship of Karl Rahner. It is, needless to say, an invaluable book. In the Rahner editions, care has been taken to indicate in the final index those passages which are "more solemn." These are usually defined statements. Those not so indicated are referred to as "implicitly or imperfectly containing important material."[2] The sections on sacraments in general which Denzinger presents as the solemn, official statements are as follows:

1. Certain sections of the Council of Trent, namely the canons, promulgated by the Council, 1547–1563.
2. Certain passages from the *Decree for the Armenians,* "Exsultate Deo," promulgated on November 22, 1439.

Other statements, contained in this *Enchiridion* are not considered "more solemn," but rather "implicitly or imperfectly containing important matter." Let us consider the statements from the Council of Trent first, which for the most part are quite clear. One preliminary *caveat* is in order, however: the canons begin with the phrase, "If anyone says ... " and end with the formula, "Let that person be anathema." Jedin, who as mentioned above is probably the main expert on the Council of Trent in our century, notes regarding this "anathema": "The canons, with their appended anathemas, are not to be regarded without more ado, as so many definitions *de fide definita.*"[3]

In the area of sacraments in general, we are dealing with the deliberations of the Council of Trent from January 15, 1547 down to March 9, 1547. During this time, Paul III was the Pope, but he was in Rome, not in Trent. The sessions of the council were moderated by his legates: Cardinal Giovanni Maria del Monte, who later became Pope Julius III, and Cardinal Marcello Cervini, who later became Pope Marcellus II. In attendance, besides these two cardinals, there was one other cardinal, nine archbishops, fifty-two bishops, two procurators for two absent bishops, two abbots, and five major prelates of religious orders, namely, the generals of the Dominicans, of the Conventual Franciscans, of the Hermits of St. Augustine, of the Carmelites and of the Servites. In total, at these sessions, seventy-one prelates were in attendance—a small number, indeed.

Besides these official voting members, there were also officially appointed theologians: Dominicans, Observant Franciscans, Conventual Franciscans, Augustinians, Carmelites, Servites and Diocesan. There were present as well in an official capacity some representatives of the nobility and other lay leaders.

Because of the small number of official delegates, the bishops were not anxious to overstep their prerogatives, lest in the eyes of the Christian world the entire validity of the council would be called into question. Since the atmosphere was so different from that of either Vatican I or Vatican II, one must appreciate the caution that the prelates at the Council of Trent exhibited. Other factors also played a role in creating a tense atmosphere: Paul III frequently informed his two legates, Del Monte and Cervini, not to tolerate any lessening of papal power, even in small matters, and the two delegates had to protect papal prerogatives along a wide front. At the other end of the power struggle was the emperor who was jockeying for his own prestige and power. If a split came between Pope and emperor precisely at that time of history, the fragile peace of Europe might be broken and damage would be done to both the papacy and to the empire. The French factor in the curia at Rome, however, delighted in the insecurity of the council, since a breakdown of the council would have diminished the power of the German emperor and strengthened the French political power. Moreover, a lessening of papal power would provide greater power to the curia. The bishops at the Council of Trent felt that the Roman curia had little if any interest in reform movements, particularly if such reform movements affected the curia itself. All of these pressures indicate that the prelates at Trent were endeavoring to keep the roof from collapsing and were, in the main, very cautious.

This caution shows itself in the council's refusal to handle some matters. For instance, there was a small minority which wanted to condemn the writings of the reformers by name. In the draft of errors on the sacraments proposed, but never adopted, for discussion on February 26, 1547, we read:

> These and other similar statements which have been noted by some of the council fathers are omitted hereby, lest we would draw up a decree in the form of a tome; rather, we have taken care that the main articles are condemned, leaving the others to be condemned later, since all the books of the heretics will be condemned.[4]

Wholesale condemnation of books was rejected by the council, since such a blanket condemnation would call into question the very validity of the council.

Instead, the men at Trent devised a new method to handle the material. In the preceding session of the council, session 6, in which the *Decree on Justification* was formulated, there was a fairly lengthy presentation on the Catholic view of justification, pastoral and didactic in nature, followed by the more polemical canons. For the sacraments, the legate Cervini suggested that excerpted statements from the reformers' writings themselves be culled out and condemned. The loudest opposition to this came from Bishop Archinto of Saluzzo, the vicar general of Rome, who suggested in his response of February 12, 1547, that the pattern of the Council of Florence be followed, namely, that a small compendium of the Catholic faith on the sacraments be drawn up for acceptance by all Catholic Christians. His suggestion was likewise not accepted by the council—and with good reason. In the matter of sacramentality, even though a very developed theology of sacraments had been formulated by the time of the Council of Trent, there were still serious issues which divided the Dominican and Franciscan theologians. It is noteworthy how many times the legates had to remind the bishops that they were at a council not to settle the theological disputes between the schools (Dominican and Franciscan) but to condemn the erroneous statements of the reformers. Since this left many sacramental issues open questions within Catholic thought, a compendium called *The Catholic Teaching on the Sacraments* was not even seriously considered.

This background material hopefully helps us to read the council documents in a more enlightened way. The material is quite pastoral in nature, insofar as the bishops wanted to present guidelines for preaching and teaching. The documents they put together had no intention of settling disputed matters within the Catholic family of scholars. The canons were outward-looking, i.e., they were focused on the reformers' teachings which the council judged incompatible with Catholic thought. Men like Seripando, Le Jay, Bonuccio, Campeggio—all articulate leaders during the council proceedings—were most cautious about the wording of these canons, for they above all had read and reread the reformers' writings. Nonetheless, as the drafts went through one formulation to the next, the precise wording was often changed for the sake of clarity, to the point, naturally, that the canons no longer cited the reformers' wording verbatim. Even, at times, this sharpening of the text in its various draftings came to express a position which would be most difficult to find in the writings of the reformers.

It is against this background that Jedin's statement, alluded to above, makes better sense. Let me cite the passage at length:

> It should be observed that at this time the anathema had not yet entirely lost its disciplinary character; it was still a formula of excommunication. For this reason, it was all the more easy to refrain from a nominal condemnation of Protestant authors. The prelates and theologians of the Council, above all Cardinal Cervini, still entertained a somewhat wider conception of faith and heresy than that elaborated by modern theology. Hence, the canons, with their appended anathemas, are not to be regarded without more ado as so many definitions *de fide definita;* what they do is to express the fact that a specific doctrine is in formal opposition to the faith proclaimed by the Church, so that whosoever maintains such a doctrine denies her teaching authority and thereby separates himself from her.[5]

Seripando, in a response dated February 16, 1547, wrote in a quite similar vein: "All the articles which are proposed are to be condemned as heretical, since they are heretical due to the fact that they go against the practice of the Roman Church."[6] In other words, the heresy might not be in the doctrine per se, which someone claims, but in the contumacy against the legitimate authority of the Church. Care and good solid historical research must be taken in this matter.

Perhaps it is for this reason that the manuals of theology, those textbooks used in seminaries for so many decades, did not present their materials with a simple restatement of a council statement. Generally, these textbooks reworded the material into the form of a *thesis*. The full council statement was cited in the body of the article under consideration to indicate the *valor* of the thesis, e.g., *de fide definita*. It is also noteworthy that even though the Denzinger volume has been available since 1854, it was not used as a text either, but as a reference work.

This last comment applies to similar books in English, such as *The Teaching of the Catholic Church*, edited by K. Rahner,[7] or *The Church Teaches*, under the editorship of J. F. Clarkson, J. H. Edwards, W. J. Kelly and J. J. Welch, Jesuits on the faculty of St. Mary's College in Kansas.[8] All of these kinds of books present documents, either in the original languages or in translations, of important Church pronouncements. The majority of the statements gathered in these books are not solemn, official teachings of the Church, but, as we noted in the Denzinger volume, statements which implicitly or imperfectly contain important material.

Let us consider now the *Decree for the Armenians* promulgated in 1439. This decree is based on a small work of St. Thomas Aquinas, *De articulis fidei et Ecclesiae sacramentis*. The authorship by St. Thomas already raises a note of caution, since, as we saw above, even the Council of Trent did not want to side with either the Dominican school or the Franciscan school in theological matters, which these two schools disputed. Since the *Decree for the Armenians* at times sides with a Thomistic position on sacraments, which in no way is the official teaching of the Church on the matter at hand, scholars must be quite circumspect in the way in which

they deal with this decree. Even though it is difficult to pin-
point in the decree solemn, official Catholic teaching on the
sacraments, the decree remains a highly important document. One must simply be apprised of its background and
handle the decree with legitimate caution.

Let us now consider the official statements of the Church
which we can consider *de fide definita.* There are only nine
such instances.

1. The Sacraments Are Instituted by Christ

This is the traditional language, used at the Council of
Trent, to indicate that the sacraments are not of human origin, but of divine origin. This is clearly the issue which is at
the heart of this doctrine: God's action, not human action, ac-
counts for Christian sacraments.

Protestant Churches should have no difficulty with this
teaching, since Luther and Calvin agreed with the Roman
Catholics on the definition of sacrament. Throughout Chapter Fourteen of his *Institutes of the Christian Religion,* Calvin stresses that sacraments come from God.[9] Luther is no
less insistent on this matter. The argument between the reformers and the Roman Church was on the number of such
sacraments and on the way that the sacraments bring about
grace. Luther and Calvin maintained that the New Testament only indicated two sacraments instituted by the Lord;
the Roman Catholic position was that there were seven. Luther and Calvin maintained that the other five sacraments
were of human origin; the Roman Church asserted that they
were also of divine origin. The application as to number was
the area of disagreement, not the clear understanding that
sacraments come from God and not from human resources.

In one of the better manuals of theology, *Sacrae Theologiae
Summa,* put out by the Jesuits of Spain, Joseph de Aldama,
in his discussion on this issue, notes that the "institution by

Christ" is *de fide divina et catholica definita,* but that this was accomplished by Christ, insofar as he was human, is simply a more common opinion among Catholic theologians. In other words, the divine origin is the thrust of this "institution by Christ," not the human origin, not even the origin of sacraments from the human nature of Jesus.[10]

2. Sacraments Are Symbols of Sacred Things

In speaking of the Eucharist, the Council of Trent, in its opening chapter, cites a definition of sacrament, found in the decretals of Gratian: namely that a sacrament is "a symbol of a sacred thing and a visible form of invisible grace." Actually, this definition is a compilation of St. Augustine's definitions: "a visible sign of a sacred thing" and "a visible form of an invisible grace."

This official and solemn teaching stresses that sacraments have as their reality something divine. The reality of the sacraments is transcendent. This is the focus of the teaching. In sacraments we are not dealing with something created, but with God himself.

Again, Luther and Calvin found no problem with this kind of language nor with this kind of teaching. Both cite Augustine in a positive way, so that we can say today in our ecumenical dialogues that this kind of understanding of a sacrament is not an issue of division. Indeed, the traditions of the Roman Catholics, the Orthodox, the Anglicans, the Lutherans, the Calvinists and many other Protestant groups have consistently maintained this kind of teaching on sacrament.

3. There Are Seven Sacraments

This was clearly stated at the Council of Trent, and at that time Calvin, Luther, Zwingli and others were maintaining that there were only two sacraments: baptism and Eucharist. The Roman Catholic teaching, expressed officially at the council, was aimed primarily at this reduction. However, some issues need to be considered.

(a) It was only about the time of Peter Lombard (ca. 1100–1160) that marriage was accepted as a sacrament of the Church and the sevenfold number was reached. Prior to that time there was strong resistance by theologians and bishops to marriage as a sacrament. If we go beyond the twelfth century, into the eleventh century or the tenth century and so on, it would be impossible to find a teaching on "seven sacraments." Likewise, the further back in history we go from the eleventh century, confirmation as a separate sacrament becomes problematical. Indeed, prior to 150 A.D. we have *only* historical data on baptism and Eucharist. Historically, then, we cannot say that "seven sacraments" has been a teaching of the Christian Church "from the beginning."

It is one thing to say "dogmatically" that there are seven sacraments; it is another thing to say "historically" that there are seven sacraments. History, it seems, will not bear out a continuous Church teaching on this matter. Since this history of the sacraments is fairly new, an acceptable agreement between the dogmatic and the historical has, as yet, to be worked out in detail.

(b) Vatican II has stated clearly that the Church is a basic sacrament, and the teaching of many respected Catholic theologians today is that Jesus in his human nature is the fundamental sacrament. Were one simply to take a numerical count, we would find that there are now nine sacraments. In dealing with the Church as a basic sacrament the bishops at Vatican II did not feel in any way that they were opposing the teaching of the Council of Trent on the sevenfold number of sacraments. Catholic theologians also do not feel that they are opposing Church doctrine, when they describe both Jesus and the Church as basic doctrines.

In the one instance (a) we have the history of sacraments *prior* to the Council of Trent, which does not uphold a teaching on seven sacraments; in the other instance (b) we have the history of sacraments *after* the Council of Trent, which in our day speaks of Jesus and the Church as sacraments. Evidently, some modification needs to be made to accommodate both (a) and (b). I would suggest the following.

What is clear is this: at the time of the Reformation the Roman Catholic Church held that there were seven sacraments and these were named individually in official documents as well as in theological treatises. This was the teaching and the practice of the Church at that time. The council said nothing about the situation prior to Peter Lombard, when the seven sacrament doctrine was neither the teaching nor the practice of the Church, and nothing was said to preclude a Vatican II from speaking about the Church as a basic sacrament. To oppose the sevenfold number of the Church's sacraments, in the sixteenth century, was to oppose the authority of the Church. Jedin's comments cited above on the meaning of "anathema" and "heresy" at the time of the Council of Trent finds application here, at least it seems to me. In addition, the Council of Trent clearly stated that all the seven sacraments are not of the same rank and dignity ("inter se paria ut nulla ratione aliud sit alio dignius, a.s.") [can. 3]. Baptism, and above all Eucharist, enjoy a far greater dignity than the other sacraments. Today, Jesus and the Church, as sacraments, enjoy a far greater dignity than all seven sacraments, including baptism and Eucharist. The teaching on the sevenfold number of sacraments is not nullified or voided, but with the historical material we have today and the newness of sacramental thinking which comes from Vatican II, some nuancing and contextualizing is clearly in order.

4. Sacraments Confer Grace

In this teaching of the Church the main issue is, once more, the transcendent aspect of the sacraments. Sacraments are neither idle signs, conferring nothing, nor merely human signs, conferring only something human. In the sacraments God is at work.

That God acts in the sacraments is not a source of division among the Christian Churches. The division arises in the "how" of this "conferring." We considered the various theological positions in the chapter on the causality of the sacraments, and it was noted there that the Council of Trent did not close the Scholastic disputes on this matter. These differences remain open questions, and all the theories put forward retain legitimate character.

There is a deeper issue beneath this statement: sacraments confer grace, and this deeper issue is the relationship of grace and good works. At this deeper level there is clearly division among the Christian Churches. Clearly, sacramental action is a good work, but in what way is this good work related to God's gift, grace? Is it magical? Is it mechanical? Is it manipulative? When the Catholic Church, at the time of the Council of Trent, spoke of the sacraments acting *ex opere operato,* was this constraining God in any way? When it spoke of *ex opere operantis,* what kind of good work was envisioned? In the *Decree on Justification* the Council of Trent clearly maintained the freedom and sovereignty of God. Justification is a grace of God, and cannot be magically, mechanically or manipulatively wrought from God by us. The same is true in the Catholic Church's teaching on the sacraments. In a very circumspect way, the Council of Trent states that sacraments do not confer grace simply because of "human faith" [can. 5]; sacraments indeed do confer the grace which they signify [can. 6]; and they do this if there are no human obstacles [can. 6]. Indeed, the council states clearly the reason for such conferral of grace: God has ordained this [can. 7] "quantum est ex parte Dei." The council emphasizes this free action of God in its use of the term *ex opere operato,* in contrast to the human good work: the human side of faith [can. 8].

When theological positions on instrumental, efficient

causality or moral causality or even occasional causality are used to "explain" the council statements, unclarity arises. The council statements in a very terse way simply state:

1. God acts through the sacraments to give his grace.
2. Humans can set obstacles (i.e., sin).
3. The sacraments confer the grace they signify (based on Augustine's approach to visible signs).

How these three areas are put together in detail is left to theologians and to theological opinions.

5. Three Sacraments Confer a Character

Using current theological language the Council of Trent officially stated that three sacraments, namely baptism, confirmation and orders, conferred a character.

There is a long history to this statement, one that antedates the Reformation by centuries. It has to do with the question of rebaptism (and therefore confirmation is involved) and reordination of those previously baptized and ordained by heretics. From 200 A.D. onward, the Christian community had struggled with this issue. At times Churches did rebaptize and reordain those who had been baptized and ordained by heretics. At times, Churches did not do so. The debate was deep and complex and almost, at times, insoluble. Finally, however, the Christian Church concluded that there should be no rebaptism or reordination. It is this teaching which lies at the heart of the Tridentine official and solemn statement that three sacraments produce a character. Roman Catholics, Orthodox, Anglicans, Lutherans, Calvinists and many other Protestant groups have no problem with the issue of rebaptism and reordination. It simply is not done (the practice of the Churches) and it is not taught (the teaching of the Churches).

We owe much to J. Galot for his study, *La Nature du Car-*

actère Sacramentel, published in 1956. This is a detailed history of the Church's teaching on character, from Scripture, through Augustine, to the Council of Trent.[11] Galot states very clearly that the Council of Trent defined *that* there is a character, but not *what* this character might be: "Le concile définira l'existence comme certaine, mais refusera de se prononcer sur la nature du caractère."[12] Even by Trent's wording, "hoc est signum quoddam spirituale et indelibile," there was no definition of what the character might be. At the time of the Council of Trent, various theories by theologians, both Dominican and Franciscan, were being propounded. The council left all such theories open and legitimate, and that openness remains valid today.

When theologians begin to define the "what" of this sacramental character and insinuate that it is "Catholic teaching," they are clearly going beyond the limits of both good theology and adherence to the teachings of the Church.

When one sees that the teaching on "sacramental character" is essentially a teaching on non-repetition of baptism (confirmation) and orders, then its validity as official and solemn teaching of the Church is clearly visible and in the best sense ecumenical.

6. God's Action in the Sacraments Does Not Depend on the Intention or Probity of the Minister

In many ways this solemn teaching follows from the above, and for two reasons. (a) The Council of Trent did not want to make God's grace depend on human "good works," namely, the intention of the minister or his holiness. As far as the intention of the minister is concerned, the person must at least intend to do what the Church intends; otherwise, sacraments are clearly not signs of something sacred. Church ministry is part of the sign-aspect in sacraments. (b) The Council of Trent, on the other hand, did not want to make the sacraments depend on the holiness of the minister, since this was precisely the issue involved in the rebaptism and reordination struggle. Clearly, a minister of the sacraments should be holy, but human sin is not greater than divine grace. As Luther said: "Jesus is greater than Satan."

Canons 11 and 12 focus on the intention and holiness of the minister, and since these were issues which the Church had long struggled with in the cases of heretical baptism and heretical ordination, the Council of Trent fundamentally repeats what the resolution of the Christian Church on this matter was. Naturally, the bishops had in mind the situation of their own day as well. Some of the reformers claimed that the Roman Church had so distorted the meaning of sacrament that Roman priests, in their sacramental ministry, intended something against the Gospel and therefore were not true ministers of the Gospel. Likewise, the bishops and priests of the Roman Church were so far from being Gospel ministers that they were not holy and consequently distorted sacramental action. This was simply another situation of the problem which lay at the rebaptism and reordination struggle.

7. The Ordinary Magisterium of the Church

Up to now, we have been looking at some rather specific teachings of the Catholic Church which officially and solemnly have been declared. These are referred to as "infallible teachings" and have been promulgated by the "extraordinary magisterium" of the Church. It would be myopic to say that this is the sum and substance of Church teaching on the sacraments. At the Council of Trent canon 13 is quite important:

> If anyone says that the accepted and approved rites of the Catholic Church that are customarily used in the solemn administration of the sacraments can, without sin, be belittled

or omitted by the ministers as they see fit, or that they can be changed into other new rites by any pastor in the Church, let him be anathema.

This canon has a certain timeliness today, since Vatican II called for a revision of the sacramental rites of the Church, and, as we know, these new rites have been developed and promulgated. These rites are indeed official teaching of the Church. No one, however, not even the Pope or the bishops, claims that these rituals will never be changed. In this sense we cannot claim that they are "infallible." Indeed, they are quite "fallible," since at some future council the Church may call again for a renewal and revision of the sacramental rites of the Church.

To disregard these new rites, however, is to go against the ordinary magisterium of the Church and to do so contumaciously is to impugn the authority of the Church. The Anglican Church in the United States has revised its *Book of Common Prayer*. Many Lutheran synods in the United States have developed a common *Manual on the Liturgy*. These volumes in a way parallel the new Roman Catholic ritual. In all of these rituals the respective Christian community is saying in an official way something about the "ordinary magisterium of the Church." Infallible statements are not directly made, but there is a clear use of ordinary authority in each case.

Canon 13 of the Council of Trent clearly states this kind of ordinary magisterium. Accepted and approved rituals are not simply items to be disregarded at whim. They are not to be belittled, omitted or changed by any pastor or priest. If one does so, and does this in formal contempt of Church authority, then, as the Council of Trent clearly states, that person is excommunicated: anathema.

Today, disregard of the new Roman Catholic ritual can be seen as an example of Trent's canon 13. To use unauthorized Eucharistic prayers and to use the Latin Tridentine Mass are both contrary to the ordinary magisterium of the Church, and if done contumaciously would indeed incur a Church condemnation.

Looked at in this way, the solemn teaching in Canon 13 at Trent on ordinary magisterium is clear and once again ecumenically meaningful.

As one notes, the Roman Catholic Church has not spoken out in a solemn and official way on sacraments in general in any lengthy and detailed way. Rather, its few statements are brief, clear and by and large noticeably traditional, in keeping with the tense and traditional atmosphere at Trent which we described above. These official and solemn statements do not present a "theology of the sacraments." They merely provide some fundamental issues on which a complete theology of the sacraments might be built. One must remember, however, that the superstructure on these few but foundational points is not defined doctrine of the Church. When one finds, for instance, that the theological description of sacraments as constituted by "matter and form" "seems to be *de fide definita*," as one reputable theologian wrote,[13] one begins to wonder about the quality of such a person's theology. When one speaks of clear, official, solemn teachings of the Church, one does not use the verb "it seems" (*videtur*). To imply without solid base that "matter and form" is defined doctrine is precisely the kind of theologizing which this chapter has attempted to restrain. Rather, we have asked in each instance what is the main focus of the official and solemn teaching. When that precise focus is clarified, many of the divisive understandings begin to give way, on the one hand, and many of the secondary theological positions (opinions) are, on the other hand, shown for what they truly are: namely, mere positions and by no means Church doctrine.

The following is an English translation of the canons on sacraments in general which the Council of Trent officially and solemnly promulgated:[14]

1. If anyone says that the sacraments of the New Law were not all instituted by Jesus Christ our Lord; or that there

are more than seven or fewer than seven—that is, baptism, confirmation, the Eucharist, penance, extreme unction, holy orders, and matrimony; or that any one of these is not truly and properly a sacrament: let him be anathema.

2. If anyone says that these same sacraments of the New Law do not differ from the sacraments of the Old Law except in ceremonies and in external rites: let him be anathema.

3. If anyone says that these sacraments are equal to one another and that one is not in any way of greater worth than another: let him be anathema.

4. If anyone says that the sacraments of the New Law are not necessary for salvation, but that they are superfluous; and that men can, without the sacraments or the desire of them, obtain the grace of justification by faith alone, although it is true that not all the sacraments are necessary for each individual: let him be anathema.

5. If anyone says that these sacraments were instituted only for the sake of nourishing the faith: let him be anathema.

6. If anyone says that the sacraments of the New Law do not contain the grace that they signify or that they do not confer that grace upon those who do not place any obstacle in the way—as if they were merely external signs of the grace or justice received through faith and insignia, so to speak, of a Christian profession by which men distinguish the faithful from infidels: let him be anathema.

7. If anyone says that, as far as God's part is concerned, grace is not given through these sacraments always and to everybody, even if they receive the sacraments correctly, but only sometimes and to some people: let him be anathema.

8. If anyone says that through the sacraments of the New Law grace is not conferred by the rite itself [*ex opere operato*] but that faith alone in the divine promises is sufficient to obtain grace: let him be anathema.

9. If anyone says that in three sacraments, namely, baptism, confirmation, and holy orders, a character is not im-

printed on the soul—that is, a kind of indelible spiritual sign whereby these sacraments cannot be repeated: let him be anathema.

10. If anyone says that all Christians have the power to preach the word and to administer all the sacraments: let him be anathema.

11. If anyone says that the intention, at least that of doing what the Church does, is not required in the ministers when they are effecting and conferring the sacraments: let him be anathema.

12. If anyone says that a minister in the state of mortal sin, though he observes all the essentials that belong to effecting and conferring the sacrament, does not effect or confer the sacrament: let him be anathema.

13. If anyone says that the accepted and approved rites of the Catholic Church that are customarily used in the solemn administration of the sacraments can, without sin, be belittled or omitted by the ministers as they see fit, or that they can be changed into other new rites by any pastor in the Church: let him be anathema.

Discussion Questions

1. What is the Church's official teaching on the issue that the sacraments were instituted by Christ? What is the precise point behind this teaching?
2. What does it mean to say that a sacrament is a symbol of a sacred thing?
3. The Catholic Church teaches at the Council of Trent that there are seven sacraments. How can one maintain that this is "official Catholic teaching," if one considers the early history of the Church and the official teachings of Vatican II?
4. What does the phrase "sacraments confer grace" mean?

What does the phrase "three sacraments confer a character" mean?

5. If a priest is not very holy, does this affect his sacramental actions? If so, why? If not, why not?

6. What is meant by the "ordinary" magisterium of the Church?

Chapter Eight

Sacraments and Christian Spirituality

THE CHRISTIAN SACRAMENTS WOULD BE INTERESTING IN some ways but not very meaningful unless the sacraments were also a profound source of Christian spirituality. In this chapter, let us consider some of the ways in which Christian sacramentality has nourished our spirituality. We will not consider in lengthy detail the individual sacraments and the ways in which these help one's spirituality. Our focus, rather, will be on the fundamental sacramental nature of the Christian faith itself. Our considerations will follow the pattern mentioned in the preceding chapters, which has been strongly advocated by the Second Vatican Council and by subsequent documents from Rome:

1. We will consider Jesus, in his sacramental humanity, as the primordial source of Christian spirituality.

2. Secondly, we will consider the Church, in its role as basic sacrament, as a fundamental source for spirituality.

3. Lastly, we will consider in a brief way the spirituality of the individual sacraments.

1. Jesus, in His Sacramental Humanity, the Source of Spirituality

It would indeed be odd if in the Christian Church the center of one's spiritual life were not Christ. Why else would one characterize this group of believers as "Christians," if Christ Jesus were not at the very center not only of its theology but also of its spiritual life? Still, what does it mean to say that Jesus is the center of Christian spirituality? Particularly, what does it mean to say that Jesus, in his sacramental humanity, is the center of Christian spirituality? It certainly does not mean that God is not at the heart of Christian spirituality, for spirituality in its deepest dimension will always be theocentric. By its very nature, spirituality is the lived experience of communion with God, a God who initiates this experience of communion and who nourishes it throughout its growth and who culminates it in what one calls the experience of "heaven." Without God, spirituality is impossible.

In the Christian approach to life, however, Jesus, the incarnate Word, has revealed to us precisely the kind of God in whom we believe and for whom we live. This does not mean that prior to Jesus no one really had an understanding of God, but it does mean that Jesus has revealed in a clearer way who and what God is all about. Jesus fulfills the law and the prophets, as we often hear; he does not overturn them. The God of the Old Testament remains the same God that we find in the New Testament, but Jesus so explains this God that new aspects of God's own life are brought to light. Indeed, one finds in the Old Testament a rich and powerful Jewish spirituality which the psalms and the prophets are eloquent in expressing. Jesus builds on this spirituality and makes it even richer and more powerful.

The key for all this is, of course, the New Testament's central belief that Jesus is the Word incarnate, that is, the divine in human expression. As we have seen above, Jesus, in his humanness, is the sacrament of God, and this human expression of God is found not only in a most exemplary way but in a quite unique way in Jesus' human life, death, and resurrection. No one has ever revealed God more clearly than Jesus, and, as our Christian faith teaches us, no one ever will reveal God more perfectly. Abraham, Moses, David,

Solomon all revealed something of the wonders of God; but Jesus is far greater than an Abraham, a Moses, a David or a Solomon. For a Christian, Jesus is unique, unsurpassable, central.

The Old Testament generally viewed God as Lord and Master, but there was in Old Testament thought no philosophical theologizing on God. Rather, "to know God" was fundamentally an encounter with a personal reality.[1] Yet, if one knows a person, one knows a name, and Israel's names for God were many: El, Elohim, Eloah, Shaddai, Baal, Adonai, Melek, Yahweh. However, no matter what the name might be, for Israel there was but one God, who in many ways always remained the unnamed. This one God was not only Israel's God, but the God of all the earth and all that was created: the true God of both Jew and non-Jew alike. God was the living God, the God of all life, no matter where one found it. Still, this one God of all had chosen or elected Israel in a special way, and because of this election, Israel's God was a jealous God, allowing the Jewish nation to worship no other God than the one God of all.

Jesus does not depart from this in any way, but he shows that God is much more than a Lord and Master; God is more than a God of the fathers; God is so close to each and everyone that God should really be called "Abba." This intimacy of Jesus with God, an intimacy which he urged on his own disciples, was scandalous to the Jewish leadership at the time of Jesus. "The use of the everyday word, *abba,* as a form of address to God is the most important linguistic innovation on the part of Jesus."[2] "The complete novelty and uniqueness of Abba as an address to God in the prayers of Jesus shows that it expresses the heart of Jesus' relationship to God. . . . Abba as a form of address to God expresses the ultimate mystery of the mission of Jesus. He was conscious of being authorized to communicate God's revelation, because God had made himself known to him as Father (Mt 11:27 par.)."[3] Christian spirituality, then, centers around God (theocentric) but in a way that Jesus, through his humanity, taught us: namely, that God is our Abba. In this way, Christian spirituality is Christ-centered from the very core.

The second important aspect which Jesus, in and through his humanness, revealed to us concerning God is the aspect of forgiveness. Forgiveness of sin is, of course, a vital part of the Old Testament and its spirituality, for separation from Yahweh was sin, and as such destroyed the very meaning of covenant, of election, of being with God. M. Guinan, following Noel Friedman, summarizes the covenantal theology in the Old Testament in a twofold way. There is first the covenant of divine commitment: "As a reward for an individual's virtuous behavior, God commits himself to that person and his descendants forever." We find this in the covenant with Abraham and David. "Since this type of covenant is unconditional, Israel can place great confidence in God and his forgiveness. They are sure that, even though they may be unfaithful, God will be true to his promises."[4] The second type is called the covenant of human obligation, a type which one finds with Moses. "Israel has accepted the covenant with God and is bound to live as his covenant people. . . . The prophets repeatedly called back to their covenant allegiance a people straying into the great sins of idolatry and social injustice which were the very negation of the covenant with Yahweh."[5]

Again, Jesus built on this covenantal spirituality. The kingdom which Jesus preached was a kingdom of forgiveness, but the narrowness of forgiveness that the Jewish leadership of Jesus' time had formulated was totally dismantled. If we ourselves are to forgive not just seven times, but seventy times seven, then God, who excels human nature in an infinite way, forgives seventy times seventy times seventy times seven. Jesus' message that the poor, the sinners, have God's good news of forgiveness preached to them was the major scandal in all his teaching. It undermined everything that the then Jewish high priest, scribe and Pharisee inculcated. For no other reason than Jesus' message of divine forgiveness, a message which he openly stated, challenging the then reigning religious Jewish authorities, was Jesus relentlessly pursued to his death. It is this message of "amazing grace," or "amazing forgiveness," that also centers Christian spirituality. God as a forgiving God (theocentric), but in a way far beyond anything one finds in the Old Testament teaching and spirituality, makes New Testament spirituality Christocentric.

Jesus, in the sacrament of his human life, his human death, and his human rising, reveals to us the height and breadth, the length and depth of both this Abba intimacy and this boundless forgiveness. Faced with this revelation of God, one can only stand, as great Christians have done throughout the centuries, in wonder and awe, and it is this sense of wonder, of amazement and of awe that is the beginning of prayer, and therefore the beginning of spirituality. Only when one stands overwhelmed by the loving grace of God, a grace so revealed by Jesus, that Jesus himself is seen to be truly the greatest grace of all, can one speak of *Christian* spirituality, and this spirituality is made known to us in and through the sacrament of the humanness of Jesus.

Christian experience, through the centuries, has always been a *fides quaerens intellectum:* a faith in search of genuine expression. Shallow faith cannot, then, have great meaning; only deep faith in the Lord discovers the meaning of life and attempts to express it. Hans Urs von Balthasar once spoke of the need for a "kneeling theology."[6] Without the theology, there is no clear expression of one's faith; without the kneeling there is no depth to what one might theologically express. The human response to God's loving and forgiving grace has been termed "faith," although faith is itself a gift or grace of God as well. Still, faith is the name which best describes the structure of one's relationship to God. It is a term found both in the Old Testament and in the New Testament, and it is likewise a term which goes far beyond the Jewish-Christian ambit.

Protestant and Catholic alike have been somewhat attuned to an intellectual approach to faith. This is often not seen in liturgical and prayer experiences of these Christian traditions. In these experiences, faith is perhaps more a matter of spiritual depth than intellectual formulation. However, when dialogue begins to ensue between Protestant and Catholic, the intellectual side of faith seems to take precedence; each side becomes defensive over the wording of religious content. In Catholic thought, faith has been described again and again in contemporary literature as the "assent of the mind to truths revealed by God, not because of their intrinsic evidence, but because of the authority of God who reveals them." Or as the *Baltimore Catechism* states it: "Faith is a virtue by which we firmly believe all the truths God has revealed, on the word of God revealing them, who can neither deceive nor be deceived."[7] Vatican I says the same thing more theologically: "And the Catholic Church teaches that this faith, which is the beginning of man's salvation, is a supernatural virtue whereby, inspired and assisted by the grace of God, we believe that the things which he has revealed are true; not because of the intrinsic truth of the things, viewed by the natural light of reason, but because of the authority of God himself who reveals them, and who can neither be deceived nor deceive."[8]

Jesus often spoke of faith, but not in such an intellectual way. He spoke to those of "little faith." He says again and again, "Your faith has saved you," or "Greater faith than this I have not found in all of Israel." Insistently, Jesus called men and women not simply to faith but to an ever greater faith, and in doing this he did not speak of faith in intellectual terms, what we might designate as the Scholastic understanding of faith. He was a Jew and he used Jewish categories in this matter of faith. One of the Hebrew words for faith is expressed in the term Amen. This was a common enough term in the religious world of Jesus' time, but Jesus used this term in a strikingly different way. Amen ordinarily was a sort of "final word," a "Certainly," an "I agree," but Jesus used it as a beginning word: "Amen, amen I say to you . . . " Such a usage is found in Mark, Matthew, Luke, Q, and

John. It is not translated into Greek, but kept in its original Aramaic form: Amen. Long before one even heard what Jesus was saying, Jesus asked that the response be "Certainly," or "I agree." The thrust of Jesus' use of "Amen" was: "Agree right now," or "Agree from the very start." How could this be? How could one consent, prior to understanding? An appreciation of the etymology of this word helps us see what Jesus implied in his usage of this term at the very beginning of his words.

Amen comes from the Hebrew root *mn* (min). Long before any of the words deriving from this root were used in a religious way, the word meant to pick up. As time went by, many of the cognate words of *mn* were used for picking up a baby and the entire process of rearing children. A child in its mother's arms is secure; the mother who holds her child also feels secure. A son or daughter well formed and raised by parental care has a sense of self-reliance and self-security. Maturity, indeed, means an ability to trust oneself, and not have the need to cling to parents. This notion of "security" or "reliability," then, is rooted in the very term "Amen." In the Old Testament, particularly in Isaiah, we find that the true Israelite was one who placed his or her entire trust in God, and the prophets, for their part, often railed against those Jewish leaders who professed a faith in God, a trust in God, but at the same time took out an "insurance policy" through agreements and covenants with neighboring nations. One who trusts God, the prophets said, trusts God in a whole and entire way—not with a "maybe" or a "proviso," and certainly not a trust which was backed up, "just in case," with a covenant or agreement with some human king or leader. Faith in God was to be a total entrustment to God and to God alone. Yahweh is, indeed, a jealous God.

Jesus' use of "Amen" follows this approach. "Not my will, but thine be done" simply expresses Jesus' message in a concrete way. Faith is not simply an intellectual assent; it is a total surrender of one's life to God. This total surrender is called for when Jesus begins his message with "Amen, amen

. . . " The true Israelite, the true follower of Jesus, stands before God first in a relationship of total entrustment, and only
then is there any intellectualizing. This is what is meant in
the Augustinian phrase *fides quaerens intellectum*. Faith is
first; the intellectual expression is secondary. This is what is
meant by Christian spirituality: we entrust ourselves to God
existentially and personally, not: we formulate an expression of our faith. A person of little faith is not someone who
tenders only little assent, but rather one who tenders only a
modicum of personal entrustment. A faith that saves is a
faith that relies totally on the saving grace of God, and not
merely in some partial or divided way.

All three of these elements are interrelated: the intimacy
of Abba, the amazing extent of God's forgiveness, and the
personal entrustment contained in biblical faith. We are
called on by Jesus to entrust ourselves so completely to God
that God is experienced as "Abba." As a child trusts its parents so wholeheartedly, we are called on to trust in our par-
enting God. This trusting faith must be so deep and so
pervasive that no sin, no matter how heinous, can elude the
mercy of God. Augustine, playing on the similar-sounding
terms *miseria* and *misericordia,* speaks of God's *misericordia*
(mercy) coming to meet us as we in our *miseria* (misery) attempt to flee from God. The picture Augustine offers us is
clearly a picture of a forgiving God, whose forgiveness is far
greater than our capability of sin. Encompassed by this intimate love of an "Abba-God" and by an incredibly forgiving
God, we can only entrust ourselves to this same God. We can
only say: "Lord, I do believe; strengthen my unbelief." This
spirituality or life of faith and love is what Jesus has revealed to us in his own life, death and resurrection: an Abba-
God, an unbounding forgiving God, a God in whom we can
only entrust our lives in a total, all-encompassing way. Our
response to Jesus can only be: "My God and my all." In the
humanity of Jesus, the very sacrament of God, we not only
see but experience this unsurpassable revelation of God. In
this we find the profound sacramental spirituality both of Je-

sus himself in his humanity and of ourselves as well in our own humanity.

2. The Church as a Basic Sacrament of Spirituality

The Church, as the mirror of Jesus, realizes its own spiritual depth, only when these same aspects of the Gospel are made actual in the ecclesial life generation of Christians after generation. The spirituality of the Church as basic sacrament can be no other than the very spirituality which Jesus as the fundamental sacrament revealed, proclaimed and lived. But we no longer live with a Jesus who walked in Palestine; we live only with a Jesus whom we experience in the sacrament called Church.

Spirituality, however, has at times been viewed as a private matter. Each person has his or her own particular spirituality. There is some viability to this approach, and a few people not only espouse this privatized approach to a spirituality but find it nourishing as well. Most humans are, however, communal and relational. Only in relationship to others do we really grow in our own humanity and realize our personal potential. Contemporary literature and philosophy have emphasized this in a very strong way. Camus, for instance, in *The Stranger* portrays Merseault as a fairly privatized individual, almost incapable of deep relationships. Merseault: a man who has no need, no interest, no longing for the transcendent. A man who finds life a series of events, happening one after the other in a very incoherent way. A man who finds no value in traditional moral and social values. A man who is as much confused by the good in the world as by the evil in the world. A man who will marry Marie if it makes her happy, even though he himself really does not love her deeply. Indifference, incoherence, mediocrity, earthiness—these are warp and woof of Merseault's absurd life.

In *The Plague,* on the other hand, the picture is altered,

since Camus realized that his portrait of Merseault in some ways justified even an Adolph Hitler. The Jesuit, Fr. Paneloux, the humanistic doctor, Bernard Rieux, the man concerned with sainthood, Jean Tarrou all find meaning in the absurdity of life only in and through relationships. As Albert Marquet wrote: "To discover that one is implicated in an adventure shared by others and that the same heartbreak establishes a complicity which it is impossible to evade—when one is called Sisyphus and carries within oneself the experience of all the Sisyphus' on earth—is to discover that one no more acts for oneself alone in the lucid revolt against the irrationality of the world than in the armed resistance to the oppression of the invader. In the individual, as in the general organized revolt, the solidarity of human beings is revealed."[9]

These comments on Camus are reinforced when one considers the logotherapy of Viktor Frankl, the *Mit-da-sein* of Heidegger, the field of perception of Merleau-Ponty. In the eyes of all these, and in the eyes of many more today, we humans are seen, indeed, as relational beings. If for no other reason, then, the Church, as a relational community, is a support group, a relational group, in which one finds meaning and identity. Were I alone in my thoughts about faith in God and prayer to God, and all others in my life did not share my sentiments, then I could either go it alone or rethink my position on the basis of these others and their views. One finds, in a group, which shares faith and prayer experience, a meaning for such faith and such spirituality. This sense of and need for relationality, perhaps, is one of the basic components of every religion, Christianity as well.

Yet there is surely more than this for a Christian. The Church, as we have seen, is to reflect the very message of Jesus, and it is this sacramentalizing of the Lord which is the major part of a Christian, i.e., ecclesial spirituality. There is no such thing as an individualized Christian spirituality; there is only a communal Christian spirituality, since it is only within the group of Christians that one finds this sacrament of Jesus. No one individual adequately reflects the Lord; the Church is by its very nature the *ecclesia*—namely, those who have been called together by the Lord. The Christian Church is never the calling only of a single individual. In Roman Catholic theology, this communal aspect is clearly a part of what is meant by tradition: a tradition which is not simply a matter of the past, but is the common heritage in which each generation in its own time and space continuum both shares and contributes, and thus enters into a network of relationships, both past and present. The New Testament itself is the written, shared tradition of many early Church communities: the community of Mark, the community of Matthew, the community of Luke, the community of John, the community of Paul, etc. These were privileged shared traditions which became canonized and called God's word. These writings in a unique and unsurpassable way offer us the revelation of God in Jesus. The dogmatic constitution on divine revelation, *Dei Verbum,* promulgated by Vatican II, notes:

> Sacred tradition and sacred Scripture make up a single sacred deposit of the word of God, which is entrusted to the Church (n. 10). Sacred tradition and sacred Scripture, then, are bound closely together, and communicate one with the other. For both of them, flowing out from the same divine well-spring, come together in some fashion to form one thing, and move toward the same goal. Sacred Scripture is the speech of God as it is put down in writing under the breath of the Holy Spirit. And tradition transmits in its entirety the word of God which has been entrusted to the apostles by Christ the Lord and the Holy Spirit (n. 9).

One finds these sacred writings and these shared interpretations in the community called Church. In this community one experiences anew God's own revelation in Jesus. Just as one finds in the light of the moon the reflected light of the sun, so, too, the Church, as we have seen, is itself the mystery of the moon, bringing to us the light of the world, Jesus. It is, moreover, only in this light of Jesus, reflected by the Church, that the individual sacraments begin to take on meaning. The individual sacraments of the Church are significant and spiritually nourishing only because they are rooted in an ecclesial dimension. Baptism is baptism within the Church; Eucharist is the sacred meal of the Church; reconciliation is not just reconciliation with God but reconciliation in the Church, etc. Whenever the basic sacramentality of the Church is disregarded, the individual sacraments begin to lose both their meaning and their power. They cease to be true sources of Christian spirituality.

As regards Christian spirituality, then, the Church presents us with the following essential elements:

1. Positively, the Church in its most profound identity presents us with the light of Jesus. Only in the Church do we truly find Jesus. By its message in both the Scriptures and its tradition, we find the light and strength needed for a secure spiritual journey.

2. Negatively, the Church through its lengthy tradition indicates to us that dark side of the moon where Jesus is not. The long experience of the Church over the centuries points out for our spiritual journey those areas which in the past have led away from the Lord. The Christian experience has not been orthogenetic, i.e., always tending in the best and most Christlike direction. The dark side of the moon is as present in the Church as the bright side reflecting the Lord.

3. The Church both positively and negatively does all this through its leadership and ministry, through its sacraments and prayer. These continually prod us to make even greater strides in our spiritual efforts.

The Church, then, is that basic sacrament or sign which both points to the reality we seek, Jesus the Lord, and indicates the darkness we should shun, that area in which the light of the world, Jesus, plays no role. In this sense, the sacramental Church strengthens and validates our spiritual life; in this way the Church-spirituality is fundamentally a Jesus-spirituality.

3. The Individual Sacraments as Sources of Spirituality

There are many sources of one's spirituality, and the individual sacraments must be seen as only one area of these sources. The Gospel message: "When did you see me naked, hungry, in prison, sick, etc.?" still remains a strong indication that in our life with others and their needs we truly find the Lord and thus grow in our spirituality. We are told in the Gospels to pray always, and our prayer life is also a major source of spirituality. But there are also moments when the Church gathers us together, and in this communal sharing we intensify our spiritual life.

In all these moments of sacramental sharing, our faith is challenged and nourished. We see only water, only oil, only bread, only wine; we hear only human words, but beneath these perceptible items we believe that the Lord Jesus acts and is present. If one says that it is easy to be part of a baptism, easy to share in a Eucharist, easy to celebrate reconciliation, then one perhaps has missed the faith-dimension of each of these sacramental rituals. At each baptism, each Eucharist, each reconciliation, our response must clearly be: "Lord, I do believe; help my unbelief!" In a rational way we do not "know" that Jesus is present in the Eucharist: we must believe that he is there. We do not see the action of Jesus in a baptism or reconciliation; we believe that Jesus is acting. Only when the sacraments stir up this faith-response can the sacraments truly be a nourishing part of our spirituality. This is the first and most important thing about sacramental spirituality: we see the sign, but we must believe in the reality.

Baptism is a sacrament which one receives only once in a lifetime. At the baptism, those who are adults are called on by the very sacramental action itself to believe. The Lord is acting in every baptismal ritual, and our belief in this action of Jesus helps draw us into the holiness of the moment. The presence of the Lord in baptism, as the Eastern theologians say again and again, is not only a holy presence, but a holy-making presence. Jesus is himself holy, but his presence among us makes us holy-by-association as well. Still, this is not the end of the baptismal action, for our baptism remains with us as we lead the rest of our life. Baptism, in a sense, sits on our shoulders, a sort of spiritual gravitational force drawing us continually to the very polarity of creation: the presence of God among us in Jesus. We are baptized but once; we live our baptism every moment thereafter, just as we are born into life once only, but live out our life thereafter at every moment we breathe.

If Jesus is really the baptized one, then in every baptism we are to search out what Jesus' own baptism means. In our baptized life, we, too, are called on to reflect the baptized Lord. In a very real sense, our Christian life is meant to be a life in which the heavens open and the Spirit descends and we hear God's voice: You are my beloved. Our very baptism and our baptized living reflect the profound meaning of Jesus' own baptism and baptized life.

Confirmation speaks to us about the Spirit. Like baptism, we receive confirmation but once, and in that ritual we celebrate the presence of the Spirit of Jesus in ourselves personally and in the Church community about us. Again, confirmation, though only once received, lives on each day as we pursue our spiritual journey, that is, our journey in the Spirit. We see here a close connection between baptism and confirmation: both sacraments are initiatory, but neither ends with the initiating rite. Every birthing is initiating, but being born lasts a lifetime.

Jesus is the confirmed one. Jesus, in his humanity, has been filled with the Spirit, and our confirmed humanity as well must reflect the Spirit-filled life of Jesus. The Spirit of God has returned, no longer simply in Jesus, but in his followers as well. Pentecost in some ways was a once-only event, but in other ways Pentecost is a continuing event. Jesus at each moment says to each of us: "Receive the Holy Spirit." It is this "gifting" of the Spirit which has provided the very name of one's following of Jesus: spirituality.

Eucharist speaks to us about the presence of Jesus. Indeed, the real presence of Jesus is the key to Eucharistic theology. It is also the key to Eucharistic spirituality. Again, we do not "see" Jesus as present; we must believe that Jesus is present in the Eucharistic meal. Every Eucharist, then, if celebrated correctly, deepens our faith in the Lord's presence. Today, however, the Church has asked us to understand this Eucharistic presence of Jesus in a richer way than ever before. Jesus, the Church tells us, is present in the gathering of the community, in the proclamation of the word, and in the banquet of bread and wine. Beyond this we must find the Lord not only in the table of the Eucharist, but in the table of the world around us. If we do not see Jesus in this table of the world, we will really not find Jesus in the table of the Eucharist; and if we do indeed find Jesus in the table of the Eucharist, we should leave the Eucharistic celebration with eyes of faith that allows us to find Jesus throughout the table of the world. There is, then, a social dimension to the Eucharist which the Church today urges us to appreciate more and more. This social dimension indicates to us that we cannot have a privatized spirituality, but rather a social spirituality, that is, a spirituality which nourishes us with the Gospel of Jesus in both the word and sacrament of the ecclesial Eucharistic celebration, so that we then return to our everyday life and bring that Gospel message to all who touch our lives. Liberation theologians have commented on the incongruity of Christians celebrating the Eucharist in their churches, but leaving the churches and remaining indifferent to the crying needs of oppression and pain all about them. It is this interrelationship of the Eucharistic table and the worldly table which reminds us that we really will not find the presence of the Lord in the Eucharist if we miss the presence of the

Lord in our brothers and sisters about us. Jesus is the present one, both at the Eucharistic meal and in the Eucharistic world.

Reconciliation is a part of spirituality which cannot be minimized. In the past there have developed pseudo-spiritualities which pit the spiritual elite over and against the spiritually depraved. Jesus, in the Gospels, is portrayed as especially harsh toward those Pharisees who thought themselves so holy, but disdained the "sinners" about them. Every spirituality must be grounded both in the promise of God's forgiving love, but also in the acknowledgement of one's own unworthiness. Some authors, such as Paul Tillich, have spoken of this as the Protestant principle: protesting in an unrelenting way against any spiritual elitism. In keeping with the Gospel, ours should be a publican spirituality, standing at the back, striking one's breast, repeating again and again: "Lord, I am not worthy; be merciful to me the sinner." The sacrament of reconciliation celebrates this kind of spiritual moment in a communal and ritualistic way. Nonetheless, one must carry *to* the penance celebration and carry *from* the penance celebration this continual need of repentance. No one should ever leave the sacrament of reconciliation feeling that somehow sin is no longer a part of one's life. Rather, one must leave the sacrament of reconciliation deeply aware of one's sinfulness, but even more deeply aware of the unbelievable forgiveness of the Lord. The new rite of penance in its introduction, a *praenotanda,* tells us clearly that Jesus' message was basically one of repentance; that the Church is indeed holy but at the same time always in need of purification; that there must be a continual, ongoing repentance in the Church in many different ways. *Semper purficanda:* always in need of purification—this is the key element in the sacrament of penance as far as sin is concerned; *semper reconcilians:* always forgiving, as far as the Lord is concerned.

Jesus is the reconciling one. He, in his humanity, is the sacrament of God's own limitless reconciliation. When we are reconciled in the sacrament of penance, we experience this loving forgiveness of the Lord, but we, too, must be like Jesus: men and women of boundless forgiveness. In the parables, Jesus reminds us of the servant who was forgiven the great debt but refused to forgive his fellow servant the little debt. This is not the way of Christian spirituality. As the Lord has forgiven us, so, too, we must forgive our debtors.

Marriage, as a sacrament, is not simply a covenant or consent between a man and a woman for a life together, but it is, as a sacrament, a union that the couple in Christ and Christ in the couple want to live out, reflecting the love of Jesus for the Church and the Church for Jesus. This is the message of that section in chapter 6 of the Letter to the Ephesians which deals with marriage. J. Dominian, in his book on marriage as a sacrament, writes:

> At the heart of the Trinity is to be found life-giving relationship. Marriage which reflects this life-giving, loving relationship is now seen to be a sacrament which unfolds over a lifetime. The minute daily events which contribute to its being are all taken up and transformed into a divine reality. There is nothing so little or so big in marriage that it does not participate in the Christ-like encounter between spouses and other members of the family. . . .

> Whilst all the sacraments contribute to salvation, and none can be excluded from the Christian life, the time is now appropriate to help the married appreciate the uniqueness of their own vocation. This is to be seen in the loving encounter between themselves, which spouses struggle to negotiate for many decades and is the origin of life for themselves and their children. It is a life of love which precedes the children and continues long after their departure.[10]

Jesus is the loving one: the one who really loves. In his humanity, he reflects the love of God: God so loved the world that he gave his only Son. Jesus loved us unto the end. Love one another as the Father has loved you. A husband and a wife, in the sacrament of marriage, not only profess their love on a single occasion, at the wedding, but carry their love for each other throughout the ups and downs of married life.

In the sacrament of marriage, the vows of the Christians who
marry reflect the love of Jesus himself, and in the life of the
Christian couple there is a marriage spirituality: a struggle
to make the love of husband for a wife and wife for a husband
a reflection of the love which Jesus himself both spoke about
and lived. Jesus is at the very heart of sacramental marriage
and marriage spirituality.

Anointing is the sacrament of the sick. Human spirituality
is the spirituality of human persons who are both healthy
and sick, alive and yet moving toward death, a Sein zum
Tode, as Heidegger wrote. The entire spectrum of human life
and dying is or at least can be a sacrament of the love of God
revealed to us in Jesus. It is this sacrament of anointing
which celebrates the presence of the Lord even in our physically difficult moments. Today's theology is somewhat at a
loss as regards this sacrament of anointing, mostly because
we have not yet developed a genuine theology of sickness.
Sickness has been seen as a passing moment of suffering
which prepares one for heaven, but this tends to make the
spiritual aspect of sickness valid only for the other side of
death. Such a spirituality is a spirituality of heaven, not a
spirituality of one's life here and now. Since Vatican II, the
Church has clearly begun to emphasize the role of sickness,
not simply that of death (extreme unction) in this sacrament
of anointing. Still, even the introduction to the new rite of
anointing vacillates on this issue of the meaning of sickness.
At one time, it is closely connected with human sinfulness (n.
2); again sickness is something we must struggle against (n.
3); but sickness also reminds us not to lose sight of the essential or higher things "and so to show that our mortal life
is restored through the mystery of Christ's death and resurrection" (n. 3). The spiritual message in this sacrament is
perhaps this: the Lord Jesus loves us when we are healthy
and when we are ill, and we Christians must love our Christian brothers and sisters, similarly, when they are healthy
and when they are ill. It is both the presence of the Lord to
the sick person and the presence of Christian brothers and

sisters to the sick person that lies at the heart of this sacrament. A spirituality which does not include the sick is certainly not a Gospel spirituality, for Jesus went about healing all who came to him.

Jesus is the healing one. Throughout the Gospels, Jesus is the healer; he is greater than sickness and greater than death. Just as Jesus, in his humanity, went about healing the sick, so, too, we as Christians both celebrate in the sacrament of anointing the healing presence of the Lord and carry a healing spirituality with us. Like Jesus, our life of holiness must be a life of wholeness.

Jesus, finally was priestly. Even more, he was, as the Letter to the Hebrews tells us, the only priest. This priestliness of Jesus centered on his sanctifying efforts. Jesus brought holiness to those whom he encountered. But perhaps the priestliness of Jesus is seen in a most dramatic way in the washing of the feet, at which Jesus, the very Lord of all, says: "I have not come to be served, but to serve." Jesus was the servant of holiness.

All Christians are priestly in a very real way, and thus all must carry the water and towel with them on their spiritual journey. They must get up from the table and put on the apron and wash the feet of those about them. Christian spirituality is in its deepest sense a servant spirituality, since the Lord himself was a man of service.

In a more public way, the ordained ministers must be such servants of the serving Lord. The towel and the water must be evident in their public, ordained ministry. When they are served, these ministers hide the Lord from their fellow Christians; when they serve, they manifest the Lord to their fellow Christians. There is no "ordained" spirituality which is different from the "unordained" spirituality. Whether ordained or unordained there is only this servant spirituality, this Jesus spirituality, for it is Jesus alone who is the priestly one.

The spirituality of the seven sacraments, then, is a spirituality which returns again and again to Jesus as the primordial sacrament: primordial baptism, primordial confirmation, primordial reconciliation. This Jesus makes all the sacraments Christocentric. But since Jesus, in his humanity, is the sacrament of God, all sacraments and their spirituality are ultimately theocentric. Spirituality is the journey to God, but for a Christian it is a journey mapped out and signed by individual sacraments, by the sacrament of the Church, but above all by the sacrament of the humanness of Jesus, the Lord.

Discussion Questions

1. What does the word "spirituality" mean to you?
2. What does this chapter say about Christian spirituality?

   In what way is Jesus central to Christian spirituality?
3. How does the Church encourage Christian spirituality?
4. How is Jesus, the primordial sacrament, central to the spirituality found in the seven sacraments?

EPILOGUE

THE PRECEDING CHAPTERS HAVE DEALT WITH A FEW ITEMS OF major concern as regards a general theology of the sacraments. However, only an in-depth study of each sacrament, including Jesus in his humanity and the Church, will provide an adequate basis for sacramental theology. The above material in many ways simply sets the stage for such an in-depth study.

Chapter one focused on those areas which in contemporary sacramental theology have played a major role in the renewal of sacramental thinking. Without an appreciation of these factors, the current renewal, particularly the renewal of the *rites* of Roman Catholic sacraments, and the reasons for changes do not make sense.

Chapter two offered a brief background sketch of the origin of the name sacrament and its function. The Christian Church did not begin with "sacraments." It began with baptism and Eucharist in a rather definite way, and only in time did theologians develop an overarching sacramental program and theory.

Chapter three took up the question of method. Many methods are involved in any theological discussion and no one method is sufficient. In the case of sacraments, this is particularly true since biblical material is involved, a great deal of historical material is currently being developed on each of the sacraments, and in our day and age a decided effort to involve the sacraments in human, phenomenological activity is stressed. Moreover, the Christological method has been promoted, even in official Church documents.

Chapter four is perhaps at the crux of all sacramental theology. In the recent past the difference between Catholic and Protestant sacramental thinking tended to focus around the number of sacraments, but when one studies the sacramental questions more deeply, the issue of grace and good works surfaces in a central way. "Causality" in the sacraments is but one instance of this relationship between grace and good works. If ever this issue can be resolved in an ecumenical way, the sacramental differences between the Christian Churches would for the most part disappear.

Chapter five is simply a brief statement on a most contemporary issue: Jesus in his humanity as primordial sacrament. This issue has not yet permeated Church life, and much more discussion and study on this Christological base are needed. Hopefully, more Protestant theologians will take up this issue, since to date it has remained almost exclusively a Catholic issue.

Chapter six presented a position which is proposed by the ordinary magisterium of the Church, namely, that the Church itself is a basic sacrament. Once again, however, in spite of this authority by the highest Church bodies, the idea of the Church as a sacrament is still not fully incorporated into the Church's approach to sacraments at the pastoral level.

Chapter seven dealt with the official and solemn teaching of the Catholic Church on the matter of the sacraments generally. One must clearly perceive the "heart of the matter" in each of these statements in order to appreciate both what they intend and what they leave to theological discussion.

Chapter eight, the final chapter, discusses the sacraments from the standpoint of Christian spirituality. Jesus, in his sacramental humanity, must be the central and controlling aspect not only in developing Christian spirituality but in developing a spirituality which is focused on and nourished by each of the separate sacraments.

Only a beginning has been made in this volume. Sacramental theology remains currently in a growth period, one that we can call both revolutionary and traditional. Further study will integrate the radicalness of Jesus and the Church as sacraments into the traditional sacramental life of the Church. Moreover, further study on the history of the sacraments will help us move beyond the limits of Scholastic sacramental theology into those greater areas of a Church whose catholicity is all-embracing.

NOTES

CHAPTER ONE: CURRENT ROMAN CATHOLIC THEOLOGY OF
THE SACRAMENTS

1. H. C. Lea, *A History of Auricular Confession and Indulgences
in the Latin Church* (Philadelphia: Lea Brothers & Co., 1896).

2. Boudinhon, "Sur l'histoire de la pénitence, à propos d'un livre
récent (celui de Lea)" *Revue d'histoire et de littérature religieuse,* 2
(1897), pp. 306–344, 496–524.

3. F. X. Funk, "Zur altchristlichen Bussdisciplin," *Kirchenges-
chichtliche Abhandlungen und Untersuchungen,* Vol. I (Paderborn:
F. Schoningh, 1896), pp. 155–209.

4. P. Battifol, *Etudes d'histoire et de théologie positive* (Paris: V.
Lecoffre, 1902).

5. E. F. Vacandard, *La pénitence publique dans l'Eglise primi-
tive* (Paris: Bloud, 1903).

6. P. A. Kirsch, *Zur Geschichte der katholischen Beichte* (Wurz-
burg: Gobel & Scherer, 1902).

7. F. Loofs, *Leitfaden zum Studium der Dogmengeschichte,* 4th
ed. (Halle, 1906; reedited by K. Aland, Tübingen, 1959).

8. Gartmeier, *Die Beichtpflicht, historische-dogmatisch darges-
tellt* (Regensburg: G. J. Manz, 1905).

9. P. Pignataro, *De disciplina poenitentiali priorum Ecclesiae
saeculorum commentarius* (Rome: Typographia Juvenum Opificum
A. S. Josepho, 1904).

10. Di Dario, *Il sacramento della penitenze dei primi secoli cris-
tiani* (Naples, 1904).

11. P. Galtier, *L'Église et la Rémission des Péchés aux premiers
siècles* (Paris: Beauchesne, 1932); *De Paenitentia: Tractatus dog-
matico-historicus* (Rome: Gregorian University, 1956). This is the
last revised edition of a work which he began in 1923.

12. B. Poschmann, *Busse und Letzte Ölung* (Freiburg i. B.: Her-

der, 1951); trans. into English by F. Courtney, *Penance and the Anointing of the Sick* (New York: Herder and Herder, 1964).

13. A. D'Ales, *L'Edit de Calliste: Etude sur les origines de la pénitence chrétienne* (Paris: Beauchesne, 1914).

14. K. Adam, *Die kirchliche Sündenvergebung nach dem heiligen Augustin* (Paderborn: F. Schoningh, 1917); *Die geheime Kirchenbusse nach dem heiligen Augustin* (Munich: J. Kosel & F. Pustet, 1921).

15. J. A. Jungmann, *Die lateinische Bussriten in ihrer geschichtliche Entwicklung* (Innsbruck, 1932).

16. K. Rahner, "Vergessene Wahrheiten über das Busssakrament," *Schriften zur Theologie,* Vol. 2 (Einsiedeln: Benziger, 1964), pp. 143–183. Originally written in 1953.

17. W. Bausch, *A New Look at the Sacraments* (Mystic: Twenty-Third Publications, 1983).

18. J. Martos, *Doors to the Sacred* (Garden City: Image–Doubleday, 1982).

19. D. Petau, *De poenitentia vetere in Ecclesia ratione diatriba* (1622); *De poenitentia publica et praeparatione ad communionem* (1644), reprinted in *Opus de theologicis dogmatibus,* ed. J. B. Thomas (Barri-Dueis: L. Guerin, 1870).

20. Jean Morin, *Commentarius historicus de disciplina in administratione sacramenti poenitentiae* (Paris: G. Metvras, 1651).

21. Otto Semmelroth, *Die Kirche als Ursakrament* (Frankfurt am Main: Josef Knecht, 1953).

22. K. Rahner, *Kirche und Sakrament* (Freiburg: Herder, 1961).

23. E. Schillebeeckx, *Christus, Sacrament van de Godsontmoeting* (Bilthoven: H. Nelissen, 1960); trans. into English by C. Ernst, O.P., *Christ the Sacrament of the Encounter with God* (New York: Sheed and Ward, 1963).

24. Cf. on this matter of Vatican II and the understanding of the Church as a basic sacrament: *The Ecclesiology of Vatican II,* by Bonaventure Kloppenburg, trans. into English by M. J. O'Connell (Chicago: Franciscan Herald Press, 1974); and the *Commentary on the Documents of Vatican II,* Vol. I (New York: Herder and Herder, 1967) with essays by such authors as Gerard Philips, Aloys Grillmeier, etc.

25. *Code of Canon Law: Latin-English Edition* (Washington, D.C.: Canon Law Society of America, 1983), pp. 317–319.

26. *Baptism, Eucharist and Ministry* (Geneva: World Council of Churches, 1982).

27. Sacred Congregation for the Doctrine of the Faith, *Instruction on Certain Aspects of the "Theology of Liberation"* (Vatican City: Vatican Polyglot Press, 1984); *Instruction on Christian Freedom and Liberation* (Washington, D.C.: USCC, 1986).

28. J. L. Segundo, *The Sacraments Today,* trans. into English by J. Drury (New York: Orbis, 1974).

29. J. Sobrino, *Cristología desde américa latina* (Mexico City: Centro de Reflexión Teológica, 1976), trans. into English by J. Drury, *Christology at the Crossroads* (New York: Orbis, 1978).

30. J. Sobrino, *Jesús en América Latina* (San Salvador: UCA/ Editores, 1982).

31. L. Boff, *Jesucristo y la Liberación del Hombre,* trans. into Spanish by F. Cantalapiedra (Madrid: Ediciones Cristiandad, 1981). The first part of this work was trans. into English by P. Hughes, *Jesus Christ Liberator* (New York: Orbis, 1978).

CHAPTER TWO: THE NAMING AND FUNCTION OF SACRAMENT

1. Cf. M. Barth, *Ephesians,* Vol. 2 (Anchor Bible) (Garden City: Doubleday & Co., 1974), pp. 607–753. Also, J. Grassi, "The Letter to the Ephesians," *Jerome Biblical Commentary* (Englewood Cliffs: Prentice-Hall, 1968), p. 349.

2. On this matter cf. R. Schulte, "Die Einzelsakramente als Ausgliederung des Wurzelsakraments," *Mysterium Salutis,* Vol. IV/2 (Einsiedeln: Benziger, 1973), pp. 83–86.

3. Ibid., pp. 86–93.

4. Ibid., p. 89. Schulte bases his summary of Augustine on G. Van Roo, *De Sacramentis in Genere.*

5. Ibid., p. 105. It is particularly in the *Etmologia* of Isidore that one finds clear references to the anamnesis character of the sacraments.

6. Cf. M. Heidegger, *Being and Time,* trans. J. Macquarrie and E. Robinson (New York: Harper & Row, 1962), pp. 51–52. A lengthier presentation of this entire issue can be found in K. Osborne, "Jesus as Human Expression of the Divine Presence: Toward a New Incarnation of the Sacraments," *The Sacraments: God's Love and*

Mercy Actualized, ed. F. Eigo (Villanova: Villanova University Press, 1979), pp. 29–57.

7. On the position of John Duns Scotus, cf. *Duns Scotus on the Will and Morality,* selected and translated by Allan B. Wolter (Washington, D.C.: The Catholic University of America Press, 1986) pp. 19–20, 56–57 of Wolter's introductory material, and pp. 254–262 for the text itself (both Latin and English) from the *Ordinatio.* Scotus likewise took up this theme in an earlier work, *Lectura,* but it was by no means an original question: Peter Abelard seems to have raised the issue for the first time and propounded a form of necessitarianism, which found an echo in Leibnitz.

8. Cf. Osborne, op. cit., pp. 35–36.

9. On this issue of the principle of sacramentality, one will find a more detailed sketch in K. Osborne, "Ministry as Sacrament," *Ecclesia Leiturgia Ministerium* (Helsinki: Loimaan Kirjapaino, 1977), pp. 103–118.

10. P. Tillich, *Die sozialistiche Entscheidung,* in *Gesammelte Werke,* Vol. 2 (Stuttgart: Evangelisches Verlagswerk, 1962), p. 223.

11. P. Tillich, "Rechtfertigung und Zweifel," *Gesammelte Werke,* Vol. 8, p. 85.

12. Osborne, op. cit, p. 115.

CHAPTER THREE: METHODOLOGY AND THE CHRISTIAN SACRAMENTS

1. An earlier and to some degree more expansive essay on sacramental methodology is K. Osborne, "Methodology and the Christian Sacraments," *Worship,* Vol. 48, n. 9, pp. 536–549; reprinted in *The Sacraments,* ed. M. J. Taylor (New York: Alba House, 1981). This latter volume includes some excellent essays on sacraments in general by J. Nolan, J. Wicks, J. D. Crichton, J. Empereur and K. Rahner.

2. R. Schulte, op. cit., p. 53. K. Rahner, *The Church and the Sacraments,* p. 38, speaks of the Scholastic understanding of the relationship of body to soul: the body is the sign of the soul. If this were applied to Jesus, then only his body would be the primordial sacrament of the soul, which is then the "even-more" primordial sacrament of the divine. It is actually the full humanity of Jesus, which

includes his bodiliness and his spiritual nature, that is the one primordial sacrament of the divine.

3. Cf. *The Rites,* "Praenotanda" to the *Rite of Penance,* p. 341.

4. G. van der Leeuw, *Sakramentstheologie* (G. F. Callenback, 1949), p. 219.

5. These questions follow the revised edition of the *Baltimore Catechism,* n. 2 (New York: Sadlier, 1941), pp. 109–114.

6. Pope Pius XII, *Mystici Corporis,* nn. 19, 20, 21.

7. On the influence of Theodore of Mopsuestia on the Eucharist, cf. N. Mitchell, *Cult and Controversy: The Worship of the Eucharist Outside Mass* (New York: Pueblo, 1982), pp. 49–56.

8. The reader clearly notices that these phenomenological connections are made in a rather summary and even sweeping way. They are meant only as listing of the ways in which each of the sacraments is rooted in human nature. A detailed development of each of these points can only be done when each of the sacraments is treated individually.

CHAPTER FOUR: GOD'S ACTION IN THE SACRAMENTAL EVENT

1. *Baltimore Catechism,* pp. 39, 109.

2. J. Calvin, *Institutes of the Christian Religion,* ed. J. T. McNeill, trans. into English by F. L. Battles (Philadelphia: Westminster Press, 1960) Vol. 2, p. 1277.

3. Cf. *Suma Teológica de Santo Tomas de Aquino* (Madrid: Biblioteca de Autores Cristianos, 1957) Vol. 13, ed. and trans. into Spanish by C. Aniz, pp. 56–69.

4. Aniz, op. cit., p. 63.

5. Ibid., p. 67.

6. Cf. B. Leemin, *Principles of Sacramental Theology* (Westminster: Newman, 1956), pp. 315 ff.; cf. Aniz, ibid. pp. 59–63.

7. Leeming, op. cit., p. 315.

8. J. B. Franzelin, *Tractatus de Sacramentis* (Rome: Polyglotta, 1881) 3rd ed., p. 112.

9. Alexander of Hales, *Summa Theologica,* P. IV, q. 5, a. 5. Text is found in *De Causalitate Sacramentorum iuxta Scholam Franciscanam,* ed. W. Lampen (Bonn: P. Hanstein, 1931), p. 6.

10. Lampen, op. cit., p. 9.

11. St. Bonaventure, *Commentaria in IV Libros Sententiarum,*

critical text published Quaracchi-Florence (1882–1902) *Opera Omnia,* IV, d. 1, p. 1, a. unicus, q. 4, in Lampen, op. cit., pp. 20–32.

12. Lampen, op. cit., p. 26.

13. Ibid.

14. Richard of Mediavilla, *Commentaria in IV Libros Sententiarum,* in Lampen, op. cit., p. 34.

15. John Duns Scotus, *Commentaria in IV Libros Sententiarum, Opus Oxoniense,* text in Lampen, op. cit., 46–60; cf. also Parthenius Minges, *Ioannes Duns Scotus: Doctrina Philosophica et Theologica,* Vol. 2 (Ad Claras Aquas: Typographia Collegii S. Bonaventurae, 1930), pp. 508–515.

16. H. Jedin, *A History of the Council of Trent,* trans. into English by E. Graf (St. Louis: B. Herder Book Co., 1961) Vol. II, p. 373. The article by Iturrioz appeared in *Estudios ecclesiasticos,* Vol. 24 (1950), pp. 291–340.

17. K. Rahner, *The Church and the Sacraments,* p. 36.

18. Ibid., p. 37.

19. J. Shea, "Human Experience and Religious Symbolization," *The Ecumenist,* Vol. 9, n. 4, 1971, p. 50.

20. Herodotus, *History,* trans. G. Rawlinson, in *Great Books of the Western World,* ed. R. M. Hutchins (Chicago: W. Benton, 1952) Vol. 6, p. 202.

21. For this I am drawing on Rahner, Heidegger, Scotus and Fransen.

22. For contemporary theology on grace, cf. P. Fransen, *The New Life of Grace,* trans. into English by G. Dupont (New York: The Seabury Press, 1973); L. Boff, *Liberating Grace,* trans. into English by John Drury (New York: Orbis, 1981).

23. B. Poschmann, op. cit., pp. 171–172.

CHAPTER FIVE: JESUS AS THE PRIMORDIAL SACRAMENT

1. K. Rahner, *The Church and the Sacraments,* pp. 15–16.

2. Schillebeeckx, op. cit., p. 13.

3. Ibid., p. 15.

4. Cf. J. Jeremias, *New Testament Theology,* trans. into English by J. Bowden (New York: Charles Scribner's Sons, 1971), pp. 76–121. It is important to see precisely what Jeremias is attempting to do. He is *not* trying to find a Gospel beneath the Gospels. He is trying

to find the *semitic substrate* of the Gospels, which then aids us to interpret the Gospels themselves. It is in the Gospels *as written* that we indeed have the word of God, not in any theologically developed theory. According to Jeremias, Jesus did not preach himself, i.e., the topic of his preaching was *not* his own person or divinity. The preaching of Jesus as Lord comes after the resurrection.

5. Vaillancourt, *Toward a Renewal of Sacramental Theology,* trans. into English by M. J. O'Connell (Collegeville: The Liturgical Press, 1979), p. 38.

6. Cf. Denzinger, op. cit., nn. 10–12.

7. Cf. J. N. D. Kelly, *Early Christian Doctrines* (London: Adam & Charles Black, 1965), p. 163: "The development of the Church's ideas about the saving effects of the incarnation was a slow, long drawn-out process. Indeed, while the conviction of redemption through Christ has always been the motive force of Christian faith, no final and universally accepted definition of the manner of its achievement has been formulated to this day."

8. J. Rivière, *Le dogme de la Rédemption* (Paris: Lecoffre, 1905); *Le dogme de la Rédemption* (Paris: Gabalda, 1914); *Le dogme de la Rédemption au début du Moyen Age* (Paris: Librairie Philosophique J. Vrin, 1934); plus many other books and articles on the subject of redemption.

9. G. Aulén, *Christus Victor,* trans. into English by A. G. Hebert (New York: Macmillan, 1969), p. ix.

10. Ibid., p. 93.

11. *Baltimore Catechism,* p. 34.

CHAPTER SIX: THE CHURCH AS A BASIC SACRAMENT

1. Kloppenburg, op. cit., p. 14.

2. Ibid., pp. 19–20.

3. Ibid., p. 19.

4. K. Rahner, *The Church and the Sacraments,* p. 18.

5. Schillebeeckx, op. cit., pp. 47–48.

6. The hierarchy, of course, includes priests and deacons, both permanent and transitional. Because the episcopal magisterium (Pope and bishops) seems to exclude any magisterium to priest and deacon, the leadership of the Church tends to be seen only in episcopal and papal terms, and as a result it would be the Pope and the

bishops who would manifest the sacramentality of the Church at a hierarchical level, at least in the strongest way.

7. O. Semmelroth, "Die Kirche als Sakrament des Heils," *Mysterium Salutis,* v. IV/1 (Einsiedeln: Benziger, 1972), p. 320.

8. R. Schulte, op. cit., p. 47.

9. Ibid., pp. 49–54.

10. *Lumen Gentium,* n. 8. This is a summary article of the entire first chapter and clearly raises the issue of incarnation. For that reason alone it is a key part of the constitution.

11. Grillmeier, op. cit., p. 148.

12. Ibid.

13. J. Bernardin, "The Sacramentality of the Church: The Necessary Context of the Sacrament of Penance," *Penance and Reconciliation in the Mission of the Church,* Synod of Bishops, 1983 (Washington D. C.: USCC, 1984), p. 19.

14. Grillmeier, op. cit., p. 150.

15. Kloppenburg, op. cit., p. 33.

CHAPTER SEVEN: OFFICIAL CHURCH TEACHING ON THE SACRAMENTS

1. H. Denzinger, *Enchiridion Symbolorum Definitionum et Declarationum de Rebus Fidei et Morum* (Freiburg: Herder, 1963).

2. Ibid., p. 807.

3. H. Jedin, op. cit., p. 381.

4. *Concilium Tridentinum,* ed. by Gorresgesellschaft (Freiburg: Herder, 1919), Vol. 5, p. 986/14.

5. Jedin, ibid.

6. Ambrosius Catharinus, *Concilium Tridentinum,* Vol. 5, p. 933/17.

7. *The Teaching of the Catholic Church,* ed. by K. Rahner, trans. into English by G. Stevens (Cork: The Mercier Press, 1966).

8. *The Church Teaches* (Documents of the Church in English Translation), edited by J. F. Clarkson, J. H. Edwards, W. J. Kelly, J. J. Welch (St. Louis: B. Herder Book Co., 1955).

9. Calvin, op. cit., Vol. 1, chapter 14, pp. 768–788.

10. Joseph A. de Aldama, "Theoria generalis sacramentorum," *Sacrae Theologiae Summa,* Vol. 4 (Madrid: Biblioteca de Autores Cristianos, 1962), p. 99.

11. J. Galot, *La Nature du Caractère Sacramentel* (Paris: Desclée de Brouwer, 1956).

12. Ibid., p. 231.

13. De Aldama, op. cit., p. 26.

14. The English translation is taken from *The Church Teaches,* pp. 263–264.

CHAPTER EIGHT: SACRAMENTS AND CHRISTIAN SPIRITUALITY

1. J. L. McKenzie, "Aspects of Old Testament Thought," *The Jerome Biblical Commentary* (Englewood Cliffs: Prentice-Hall, 1968), p. 737.

2. Jeremias, op. cit., p. 36.

3. Ibid., p. 68.

4. M. Guinan, *Covenant in the Old Testament* (Chicago: Franciscan Herald Press, 1975), p. 48.

5. Ibid.

6. Cf. Hans Urs von Balthasar, *Word and Revelation* (New York: Herder and Herder, 1964).

7. *Baltimore Catechism* (New York: Sadlier, 1941), p. 44.

8. Denzinger, n. 3008.

9. A. Marquet, *Albert Camus: The Invincible Summer* (London: John Calder, 1958), p. 81.

10. J. Dominian, *Marriage, Faith and Love* (New York: Crossroad, 1982), p. 261.

BIBLIOGRAPHY

Only books dealing with the sacraments in general are listed below; other books dealing with the individual sacraments are found in those volumes dealing with the individual sacraments. Only books available in English are listed below. References to works in other languages are given in the footnote material throughout this volume.

W. Bausch, *A New Look at the Sacraments* (Mystic: Twenty-Third Publications, 1983).

R. Browning and R. Reed, *The Sacraments in Religious Education and Liturgy* (Birmingham: Religious Education Press, 1985).

B. Cooke, *Sacraments and Sacramentality* (Mystic: Twenty-Third Publications, 1983).

B. Häring, *The Sacraments and Your Everyday Life* (Ligouri: Ligouri Publications, 1976).

J. Martos, *Doors to the Sacred* (Garden City: Image-Doubleday, 1982).

J. Martos, *The Catholic Sacraments* (Wilmington: Michael Glazier, 1982).

C. O'Neill, *Sacramental Realism* (Wilmington: Michael Glazier, 1983).

K. Rahner, *The Church and the Sacraments,* trans. into English by W. J. O'Hara (New York: Herder and Herder, 1963).

J. Schanz, *Introduction to the Sacraments* (New York: Pueblo, 1983).

E. Schillebeeckx, *Christ the Sacrament of the Encounter with God* (New York: Sheed and Ward, 1963).

J. L. Segundo, *The Sacraments Today,* trans. by J. Drury (New York: Orbis, 1974).

O. Semmelroth, *Church and Sacrament* (Notre Dame: Fides, 1963).

R. Vaillancourt, *Toward a Renewal of Sacramental Theology,* trans.
    by M. J. O'Connell (Collegeville: The Liturgical Press, 1979).
F. Van Beeck, *Grounded in Love* (Washington, D.C.: University
    Press of America, 1981).
G. Worgul, Jr., *From Magic to Metaphor* (New York: Paulist, 1980).

Index of Authors

Adam, K. 3
Albercius 21
Albert the Great 64
Aldama, J. 106
Alexander of Hales 55, 64
Ambrose 80
Aniz, C. 51, 52
Anselm of Canterbury 80, 81
Archinto de Saluzzo 103
Athanasius 80
Augustine 7, 12, 23, 24, 25, 31, 80, 107, 111, 112, 126
Aulen, G. 80

Balthasar, H.U. von 123
Basil 80
Battifol, P. 3
Baum, G. 59
Bausch, W. 4
Bernardin, J. 96
Boff, L. 17
Bonaventure 4, 55, 56, 57, 64, 89
Bonuccio, 104
Boudinhon, A. 3

Calvin, J. 9, 49, 106, 107
Camus, E. 126, 127
Campeggio, C. 104
Cano, M. 53, 67
Cervini, M. 101, 102, 103, 104
Clement of Alexandria 81
Clarkson, J.F. 105
Cyprian 11, 12, 23, 31, 80
Cyril of Alexandria 81
Cyril of Jerusalem 81

D'Ales, A. 3
Denzinger, H. 100
Di Diario, 3
Didymus the Blind 89
Dominian, J. 135

Edward, J.H. 105

Frankl, V. 127
Franzelin, J.B. 53, 54
Friedman, N. 122
Funk, F.X. 3

Galot, J. 111, 112
Galtier, P. 3
Gartmeier, J. 3
Gilkey, L. 59
Gratian 107
Gregory the Great 80
Gregory of Nazianzen 80
Gregory of Nyssa 80
Grillmeier, A. 95, 96
Guinan, M. 122

Haughton, R. 59
Heidegger, M. 25, 27, 59, 127, 136
Hermes 5
Herodotus 61
Hincmar of Rheims 8
Hippolytus 5, 21, 79
Hugh of St. Victor 7

Ignatius of Antioch 21, 22
Isidore of Seville 23, 31
Iturrioz, D. 57

Jedin, H.	57, 101, 104, 109
Jeremias, J.	72, 73
John Chrysostom	80
John Paul II	16
Jungmann, J.A.	3
Justin	21, 22
Justinian	31
Keen, S.	59
Kelly, W.J.	105
Kirsch, P.A.	3
Kloppenburg, B.	87, 88, 89, 97
Lea, H.C.	2, 3, 5
Ledesma, P.	54
Le Jay, C.	104
Leeming, B.	50
Leo the Great	80
Leo XIII	95
Lessius	54
Loofs, F.	3
Lugo	54
Luther, M.	9, 49, 106, 107
Macquarrie, J.	25, 26
Marquet, A.	127
Martos, J.	4
Merleau-Ponty, M.	127
Mohler, J.	95
Morin, J.	4
Monte, G.U. del	101, 102
Origen	22, 80, 81
Otten, B.	54
Paul III	101, 102
Paul VI	65
Petau, D.	4
Pesch, C.	54
Peter Abelard	81
Peter Lombard	6, 108, 109
Pignataro, P.	3
Pius XII	39, 95

Plato	22
Poschmann, B.	3
Puig, I.	54
Rahner, K.	3, 10, 35, 53, 58, 59, 67, 69, 70, 71, 72, 91, 92, 100, 105
Rashdall, H.	81
Richard of Mediavilla	56
Ritschl, A.	81
Riviere, J.	80
Robert Bellarmine	87
Robinson, E.	25, 26
Sasse, J.B.	54
Schillebeeckyx, E.	10, 35, 69, 71, 72, 91, 92
Schleiermacher,	81
Scotus, John Duns	26, 56, 57
Schulte, R.	35, 93
Segundo, J.	17
Semmelroth, O.	10, 69, 92, 93, 94
Shea, J.	59
Sobrino, J.	17
Tertullian	22, 23, 31, 80
Theodore of Mopsuestia	42
Thomas Aquinas	4, 50, 51, 52, 53, 55, 64, 67, 81, 105
Tillich, P.	28, 30, 134
Tournely	54
Vacandard, E.F.	3
Vallaincourt, R.	75
Van der Leeux, G.	38
Vasquez, F.X.	53, 54
Seripando, G.	104
Welsh, J.	105
Zwingli	107